Advance Praise for Never Bullshit the Client

"Richard Ennis, long a major thought leader in investing, has given his many admirers a short book on how to build a professional firm and a series of insights into the wonderful history of institutional investing."

– Charles D. Ellis, Author, Founder, Greenwich Associates

"A wonderful personal history in the investment management field. Richard Ennis shares his experiences with splendid details that are engrossing and delightfully insightful."

– Gary P. Brinson, Founder, Brinson Partners

"*Never Bullshit the Client* hits the trifecta...short, wise and very entertaining."

– Jack R. Meyer, Founder, Convexity Capital, Former CEO, Harvard Management

Richard Ennis has been a part of the financial revolution from its early days. His memoir gives us a fascinating inside look at the characters and events that continue to transform the investment industry. A fast paced, informative and enjoyable read.

– Roger G. Ibbotson, Professor Emeritus, Yale University

Richard Ennis led the evolution, arguably the invention, of institutional investment consulting as we know it. His intellectual depth is matched by his exceptional ethical and professional standards, a fiduciary's fiduciary. His work has helped investors protect and compound capital—solving problems, doing good and changing lives along the way. The history and wisdom he offers are well worth your time.

– Ashbel C. Williams, Jr., CEO,
Florida State Board of Administration

Richard Ennis was present at the creation: O'Brien Associates and then A. G. Becker, which in the 1970s were the gathering spots for most of the people who created the modern scientific investment management business. Ennis was at both firms before founding one of the premier consulting firms in the industry. A half century later in this memoir, he looks back on his multifaceted career and concludes that the topic he wants to emphasize most is ethics. Put the client's interest first, your firm's interest second, and your personal interest last. Most of all, "Never bullshit the client." Having been the client, I appreciate the blunt advice. Read this book!

– Laurence B. Siegel, Research Foundation Director, CFA
Institute, Former Director of Research, Ford Foundation

How did we get in a situation where we see an unfolding pension crisis almost everywhere we look? Richard Ennis helps us understand how we got here, and his wise insights guide us to solve the problems. His wonderfully intimate and detailed history of the arrival of modern portfolio theory provides important perspective. Central to his work are ethics and character, the under-appreciated but critical dimensions of the stewardship of other people's money. The sections "Character Counts" and "Ethical Foundation = Business Strategy" are a must-read for trustees, consultants, and investment managers who give advice and make decisions under great uncertainty with the results not known until far into the future. What could go wrong when investment complexity is hidden in math nobody really understands and the short-term incentives are for everyone to tilt the playing field? A lot can go and has gone wrong. Richard Ennis gives us practical advice that we can and should use to do a better job. — *Stephen Sexauer, CIO,*
San Diego County Retirement Association

Richard's reach and impact is simply unparalleled in the world of institutional investments. Millions of pension participants, hundreds of professionals at the legendary Ennis Knupp, and the countless readers of the FAJ during his tenure benefited mightily from his intellect and his high ethical standards. *Never Bullshit the Client* is a fitting retrospective to preserve this man's decades-long legacy. I can think of no greater gift for the next generation, and I eagerly anticipate sharing his gift with my young finance-educated daughter.

— *Steve A. Voss, Senior Partner, Aon Investment Consulting*

"This is an inspirational story about navigating choppy investment waters with lively characters while paddling with integrity, no matter the cost." — *Jennifer Paquette, Former CIO,*
Colorado Public Employees Retirement Association

"Richard Ennis, leader, mentor, educator and investor shares his personal journey in the world of investment management during a period of volatile markets and significant industry change. *Never Bullshit the Client* is one of a kind and a must-read for both industry newcomers and veterans. He explores an area of the investment industry that receives scant public interest but influences trillions of dollars of assets. Richard reminds us of the importance of respect, integrity, forthrightness and putting the interests of investors and participants above all else. This is a story that is long overdue. Thank you, Richard, for sharing this wonderful real-life narrative."

– Joanne Hickman Dodd, Senior Vice President, Capital Group

"Richard Ennis taught me, as a client at the MacArthur Foundation, the difference between good investment consulting and bad, telling me the truth versus making me feel like I was always right. His memoir clearly reflects the dedication and impact that Richard had on the industry and the people that he influenced." *– Jim Casselberry, CIO, 4S Bay Partners, LLC*

"Richard Ennis set the standard for thinking, writing, reading and being educated about investment philosophy and asset allocation. His memoir is a breathtaking kaleidoscope of people and events over his career in this burgeoning industry we now know as asset management and consulting." *– Cynthia Steer, Director, ICMA-RC*

"This book is a must read for anyone working to build a great investment firm. There are plenty of lessons for everyone—from emerging leaders to seasoned professionals. Richard Ennis tells the reader, in no uncertain terms, what it takes to make scalable breakthroughs in the investment industry." *– John W. Rogers, Jr., Founder, Ariel Capital Management*

· NEVER ·
BULLSHIT
THE CLIENT

MY LIFE IN INVESTMENT CONSULTING

RICHARD M. ENNIS

THE CAROM PRESS
Fort Myers, Florida

*In appreciation of my father, **John M. Ennis,***

who was good enough to let me pretty much

figure things out for myself from an early age.

Profits on the exchange are the treasures of goblins. At one time they may be carbuncle stones, then coals, then diamonds, then flint stones, then morning dew, then tears.

—*Félix Lope de Vega, 1562–1635*

"Always do right. This will gratify some people and astonish the rest."

—*Mark Twain*

FOREWORD

Servant Leadership Exemplified

first came to know Richard by his writings. In my early days as an investment analyst I was routinely impressed (this has never changed) by Richard's ideas expressed through his contributions to the literature. Always provocative, always relevant, and perhaps most important, always practical. I can still remember being impacted by, and eager to implement, his useful insights on an array of portfolio matters—What is the best portfolio policy? Should I toss aside the ubiquitous style box approach to organizing managers? Should I diversify my active managers? Does the "well known" alpha in small-cap stocks really exist? The list goes on. As I read this memoir and am reminded of these papers, I am struck (and believe you will be too) by how Richard's insights remain as relevant today as when they were first written.

However, to my delight, Richard has chosen to write, not just about his remarkable roster of research, but he goes beyond this by taking us on an inspiring journey of a career—a life—driven by intellectual curiosity and helping others. By stepping back and exploring the big picture, he gives us something far more impactful. Among my favorites is Chapter 5, which describes the early days of, and the luminaries responsible for, advancing applied quantitative investing, and Chapter 6, how Richard's combination of curiosity and helping others by, as he puts it, "doing what's right," leads him and his partners to create, indeed invent, the business of investment consulting.

As we read on, we discover the real treat, something even more important and impactful, and why I urge you to read the entire memoir—what sets Richard truly apart is his natural inclination to serve others. In short, serve first, lead second. Again and again as you read this memoir you will see a man who focuses with great intensity on the growth and well-being of his community—everyone around him. For him, it seems innate. Success, driven not just by a desire for leading a healthy business, but measured by the development and success of others—in business, in life, whatever their goals. Richard inspires us to serve first and to make that the foundation upon which all other principles rest—leadership and results will follow. This serve-first, lead-second mindset is plainly evident throughout this memoir, but is particularly palpable as I read Chapter 8 sections "A Nurturing yet Challenging Culture," and "Ownership." Don't miss them!

I finally met Richard in person while at CFA Institute where we worked together on the *Financial Analysts Journal* (*FAJ*). Here I experienced his supportive nature firsthand, leaving an indelible mark on my career and on my life. Perhaps the example that proves the rule, Richard, as *FAJ* Executive Editor, was chiefly responsible for contributing each issue's Editor's Corner. Rather than keep these coveted thought pieces to himself, he naturally sought to share authorship of them with the associate editor (me). When I finally got up the courage to go solo, he helped ensure my success by providing guidance until the piece was ready for prime time. To be clear, Richard never confused support for coddling; if the piece wasn't up to snuff, he would let me know gently, but unequivocally, "good start, but not quite there yet, try again," and "in your revision, don't bury the lead!" and so forth. In so doing, he challenged me to become a better thinker and communicator, but more importantly, he showed the way by example. Don't miss the section "Teach!" for more on this.

We became lifelong friends, and I am forever grateful. A person of such towering character and brilliance would have undoubtedly succeeded in whatever endeavor they chose to pursue. Too bad Occam Asset Management was never launched (see Chapter 9). I, and undoubtedly many others, would have walked through walls to be a part of such an outfit. Be that as it may, we can read *Never Bullshit the Client*. Don't miss a single word of this remarkable story. Read it, learn from it, treasure it!

Rodney N. Sullivan, CFA, CAIA
Executive Director
Mayo Center for Asset Management
University of Virginia
Darden Graduate School of Business

TABLE OF CONTENTS

Foreword I

Preface i

1. Early Life 1
2. Discovering Finance Theory 15
3. A Foot in the Door 19
4. Money Management 27
5. Early Days of Quant Investing 35
6. The A.G. Becker Years: 1975-1980 43
7. Loss of a Friend 57
8. The EnnisKnupp Years: 1981-2010 61
9. Occam Asset Management 99
10. *Financial Analysts Journal* 103
11. The Sanibel Years 109

Epilogue 113

Appendix 1 115

  A Heuristic Approach to Investment Policy 115

  Table 1: Asset Allocation of Various Types of
    Institutional Investor 119

  Table 2: Illustration of Investor Reliance
    (Risk Sensitivity) 124

Appendix 2 131

  Select *Financial Analysts Journal* Editorials 131

  Big Bond Bust 131

  Darwin and Investment Product Proliferation 136

  The Uncorrelated Return Myth 139

  Parsimonious Asset Allocation 143

  The Herd Follows the Leader 150

  Pensions or Penury? 153

  Investment Policy: Bridle of Want 156

  New Organizational Paradigm:
    A Portfolio Manager and a Band of Scouts 158

  End of an Era 163

  Hedge Fund Clones: Triumph of Form over Substance ...167

  The Investment Policy Fizzle 170

  Exploring Market Macro-Inefficiency: Call for Papers 175

Acknowledgments 179

Photos 181

PREFACE

This memoir explores my life's work. It comprises three intertwined stories.

First is a personal story beginning with my youth and some early life experiences. It moves on to my professional education, describing memorable encounters with academic legends in graduate school. The story recounts my apprenticeship in money management during the go-go years of mutual fund management. It explains my disaffection with money management and transition to consulting. It discusses my writing and consulting work. The first story concludes with my retirement and life in the years that followed.

The second story relates the evolution of institutional investment consulting from my unique vantage point. It chronicles the dawning of the quant era in the late-1960s. It recounts the formation of A.G. Becker's investment consulting business in the 1970s. It describes the founding of the first consulting effort to be recognized as a professional services firm.

The third is the story of that very special firm, EnnisKnupp. It explains the firm's business strategy as well as its ethical and professional foundation. It describes the firm's culture. It discusses the firm's research and advisory work. Finally, it relates the bittersweet sale of the firm nearly 30 years after its founding.

All three stories are replete with people, history and anecdotes that made my work life interesting for 40 years. I am grateful for the memories and my good fortune along the way.

I wrote the memoir to help people in the fields of investment management and consulting gain a better appreciation of our shared history. These stories reveal setbacks and triumphs, as well as work that remains to be done. Their telling may help the current generation, and its younger members, in particular, to make our businesses better.

> Richard M. Ennis
> Cypress Cove
> August 2019

ONE
Early Life

I was born in San Francisco during the Second World War. My family moved to Los Angeles when I was about two years old. It was a better locale for my father's law practice representing injured railroad trainmen. As a result I have no recollection of life in San Francisco. Nevertheless, I identify with the city like no other. I am rooted there.

CHILDHOOD

My attachment to San Francisco was fostered by childhood trips to visit grandparents, aunts, uncles and cousins there and in the East Bay communities of Alameda and Castro Valley. My older brother, John, and I came to know all the sights, sounds and smells that endear people from all over the world to San Francisco. Wherever the cable cars ran there was the constant rumble of the cables running underground. There was the clanging of the cars' bells as they approached. Then a tremendous leap up onto the car and hanging on for dear life. There was Fisherman's Wharf, with its famous restaurants and giant, stinky crab pots. Nearby was the Ghirardelli chocolate factory, with the distinctive aroma of roasting cocoa beans wafting from it. From the top of Coit Tower, John and I marveled at the looming Golden Gate Bridge and peered in awe at The Rock, home of notorious criminals and site of legendary escape attempts. In Chinatown the smell of incense emanated from dimly lit shops along Grant Avenue. Retiring shopkeepers and their exotic goods offered a glimpse of the mysterious Orient. At night in one of the city's storied hotels we could hear the fog horns. Their deep, sonorous "beee-OOOHH" was reassuring as we drifted off to sleep in beds not our own. These are memories to last a lifetime.

I recall an incident when Dad and I were riding in a taxi on California Street and passed the stately Pacific Union Club atop Nob Hill. It was originally the mansion of silver magnate James Clair Flood and takes up an entire block. We had a brief exchange that went something like this:

> Me, "What's that?"
> "The Pacific Union Club."
> "What are the membership requirements?"
> "There is only one—that your grandfather was a member."

Spoken without irony, that comment gave insight into my father—the successful, self-made, public school man and New Dealer, comfortable in his own skin. It also gave me an inkling of the man I might become.

I visited San Francisco many times on business over the years. Every time I did, nostalgia would well up in me such that, at this stage of my life, I do not think I would like to return.

■ ■ ■

We moved from San Francisco to Cheviot Hills, a nice area on the West Side of Los Angeles in the late-1940s. It is nestled among Beverly Hills, Century City and Palms. Dad rode the Venice Short Line (one of the Red Car light rail lines that crisscrossed the city) to his law office in the A.G. Bartlett Building at Seventh and Spring Streets in the financial district of downtown Los Angeles. He would for years be an advocate of mass transportation in a city that was doomed by the influence of Big Oil and Big Three money to become the freeway and smog capital of the world. He ran unsuccessfully but respectably for mayor of Los Angeles in 1957 on a mass-transit platform.

I attended kindergarten at Notre Dame Academy, a parochial school. (Mother was a devout Catholic, Father a wayward Presbyterian.) I had my first brush with nuns there. These were the old-school type, in billowing black habits with gigantic crucifixes on chains around their necks, oversized rosaries dangling from their waistbands and a ruler clenched in one fist. I had a reprieve when the school converted from co-ed to girls only, and I went to public school for first grade.

I made it through confirmation in the Catholic Church but lapsed not much later on. It was long enough for me to have more encounters with the nuns, mostly in Saturday catechism classes. I may have left the Church, but the sisters never seemed to fade entirely from the picture. At various times in my life I thought I got a glimpse of one standing off to the side—watching, waiting for an opening with the ruler.

The family moved to Sherman Oaks in the San Fernando Valley when I was in second grade. Sherman Oaks Elementary School was small, not far from our home and, in retrospect, almost cozy. I thrived there. By contrast, my junior high school was farther away, much bigger, more diverse and cheerless. I felt lost there.

Two noteworthy events occurred during my junior high school years. My father's law practice entered a period of decline. The giant railroads he sued on behalf of badly injured trainmen did not like being repeatedly stung in the courtroom by John M. Ennis, Esquire; so they found ways of making his specialized personal injury practice difficult. For a family that was decidedly prosperous when I was in elementary school, things became leaner. At about the same time, my mother, who I had never known to take a drink, became an alcoholic—a week-at-a-time-in-the-bedroom drunk, in fact. For his part, Dad had his hands full making a living and coping with Mother's situation.

HIGH SCHOOL

I received little parental steering in my teens. This may have been partly owing to the difficult situation at home. As or more important, though, Dad just let me be me. He was watchful and deeply caring, but not judging or controlling. That was his nature. As a result, I enjoyed an extraordinary degree of freedom in my high school years.

I got my driver's license when I turned 16. Dad bought me a car for $200. I needed one for the trip to Van Nuys High School. I got a job after school at $1 an hour to pay for the car. I went to school and worked, first in a small bottling plant and then a drugstore.

I was a math major. I had no real trouble with the subject but lacked interest in it. I do not remember any of my classes or teachers from high school. I was a good athlete but did not participate in sports or extra-curricular activities. My IQ was above average but my grades were just middling. I was well-liked and moved easily among two or three crowds, but there was no real connection with the school itself.

I developed an interest in cars. I took up smoking. I started drinking beer on Friday nights with some of my pals. We cruised Bob's Big Boy, the iconic drive-in restaurant of the era, and up and down Van Nuys Boulevard. Sometimes there was a date on Saturday night. I had one or two schoolyard scuffles to prove myself.

My interest in cars blossomed into a full-blown fascination with the workings of the internal combustion engine. I built two hot rods. I street-raced and ran one of them at San Fernando Raceway, the local drag strip. In the pits there I cheated to the best of my ability in the time-honored tradition of auto racers everywhere. It was, however, to no avail. My "D Gas" '60 Chevy simply did not have the muscle for a trophy. (Either that or the others were simply better cheaters.)

I began to frequent *Harry's*, a seedy pool hall in downtown Van Nuys near the high school. The windows were painted over, rendering it dark, save for the lights over the tables. Coffee cans served as spittoons, and the odor of stale cigarette smoke permeated the place. It looked and smelled the way a poolroom was supposed to, in other words. I became an accomplished player of 9-Ball and two-bit gambler. I learned poolroom etiquette. I spent a lot of time and money at *Harry's*.

And then one day high school simply came to an end. I don't actually have a recollection of it ending. I didn't bother attending the graduation ceremony; my diploma arrived in the mail.

I was oblivious of the future during my high school years. Could I have better channeled my curiosity and ingenuity? I suppose so. But I don't have any regrets. I spent those years in a way that made sense given the times and my circumstances. What strikes me in reflecting on those times is how profoundly grateful I am for the freedom to do what interested me. I was able to live a life of my choosing.

COLLEGE

The future arrived on the day I enrolled at Los Angeles Valley (junior) College, known simply as "Valley" to one and all. I showed up on a fall day in 1962 with the $5 registration fee in hand to begin my college education.

I went to Valley for one simple reason: Dad believed college was a good thing. I never felt pressure from him to attend college. But I knew how much he valued education. I had heard him say many times that there are two things *they* can never take away from you—your education and your good name. He lived through the Great Depression and World War Two. His father was wiped out multiple times in panics and crashes between 1907 and 1929. Dad survived for many years as a sole-practitioner litigator against powerful corporations. Thus, like many others of his generation, the *them* out there, who would take everything away from you if they could, were part of his worldview. So, as John Ennis's son and in awe of this good and noble man, and knowing not what else to do, I headed for Valley JC in 1962. It was an indication of my faith in the man. I had no idea where it might lead.

Valley proved to be my lifeline. They took anybody—like *me*: not much money, lousy grades and clueless about what I wanted to be. There I encountered a first-rate faculty, most with doctorates. I discovered Economics there. I learned to stand before a class and give a speech. I discovered that I didn't know how to write in the English language and began to rectify that. I studied Spanish and became fluent in it. I met and fell for Thoreau. I had Aristotle's definition of tragedy drummed into me. I dodged science courses. I discovered that introductory philosophy was academic rigmarole—epistemology, metaphysics, teleology. Insight into the human dilemma and the consolations of philosophy would come later, much later.

By no means did I become an academic stand-out. *Harry's* poolroom, not far away, still beckoned and was open until 2 a.m. I had graduated from the hustler's game of 9-Ball to the more cerebral game of three-cushion billiards. The table for this game is called a carom table. It is bigger than a pool table and has no pockets. There are two cue balls (one with a small black dot on it so you can tell the two apart) and one red ball. The balls, made of ivory in those days, are a bit larger and heavier than pool balls. A point is scored when you stroke your cue ball such that it strikes either of the other two, called object balls, and then careens about the table, rebounding off at least three cushions, to finally make contact with the second object ball. People say that billiards, as the game is simply known, is to pool as chess is to checkers. But seedy *Harry's* was still *Harry's,* and I continued to spend a lot time and money there.

"A proficiency at billiards is a sign of a misspent youth," goes the old saw. If this is any sort of credential in life, I earned mine at *Harry's.*

I joined a fraternity, too. Dad had been a fraternity man as well as an ice hockey player at UC Berkley before going to law school at Hastings. He encouraged me to consider joining one when I consulted him on the subject. There was plenty of beer-drinking and parties with sororities. The extraordinary thing about the fraternity, though, was the intense and enduring spirit of brotherhood that pervaded the young men of Phi Delta Psi. This existed not only among pledge classmates and other contemporaries, but across "generations" going back several years. This was the most profound experience of acceptance and bonding that any of us ever had, before or since. The older brothers would turn up at rush smokers and other special occasions in coat and tie and greet you warmly, as if we had all been together for all time. This was brotherhood, pure and simple. It continued after we were long gone from Valley and fraternities there had petered out. To this day many of us remain close, exchanging pictures of grandkids and sharing remembrances from the good old days.

Thus, there were four facets to my junior college education—books, billiards, beer and brotherhood. Speaking of "education," one summer I also had a *but I didn't inhale* experience in a Mexican whore house.

My parents appreciated my interest in the Spanish language. They arranged for me to live with a family in Guadalajara and study at the University there during my first college summer. I had never been abroad. There were four of us American students lodging and taking meals with the H. Medina family. It was a wonderful experience.

Hector and Lupe Medina had a huge, welcoming house, three small children and ample live-in help. Hector's brother Horacio became our self-appointed chaperone and guide. Horacio was unmarried, dapper and urbane. A respected attorney, he was known as *Licenciado* wherever he went in Guadalajara.

It was Horacio who took the four of us to the brothel. He was something of a prig and, I surmised, gay; but I guess he thought this would be a good experience for us. And it was. It was just like in the movies. We approached the door of a nondescript structure on a back street and Horacio knocked three times. A little peek-a-boo window opened and then the door itself. It was dimly lit and gave the impression of an Old West saloon inside. There were tables and girls to bring you drinks and talk business. But when it came time to pull the trigger, I demurred. My Catholic moral teaching with its prohibition on premarital sex kicked in and held me back. So, while the other three engaged in carnal bliss, I just sipped tequila with "my girl." I slipped her a tip so that keeping me company would not be a complete bust for her. That was it. It was a *terrific* experience. After all, how often does an upstanding fellow like me get to write about a night he spent in a whore house?

In the fall of 1963 I walked into an algebra class. A very pretty young woman—beautiful, in fact—caught my attention. She was tastefully dressed—a crisp blouse, snug skirt to the knee, hosiery and low heels. Her fair skin was set off by jet black hair pulled back in a bun. This was one hot ticket. I made a beeline for the nearest open seat. During the first week or so we exchanged pleasantries and she sold me a raffle ticket, which required me writing my name and phone number on the raffle book stub. Her name was Sally Hinton. She was quick and hip. We clicked. I asked her for a date. She was sorry, but she had a boyfriend.

Not long after that the phone rang at home. Mother answered. "It's for you," she said. "It's a young lady—Sally." I thought, *Could it be Sally Hinton calling me? Bingo!* Indeed it was Miss Hinton, calling to inform me she was no longer seeing the other young man and would be receptive to my attentions were I to call.

I arrived at Sally's mother's house on Ben Avenue in Studio City for our first date clutching a bouquet of carnations. On the front porch I rang the bell. Sally's mother answered the door and, without a word, began looking me up and down. "How do you do, Mrs. Hinton," I said awkwardly, "I'm Richard." Without breaking from sizing me up she said, not unpleasantly, "It's Goldman (she had remarried), but that's okay." After what seemed like an eternity she let me in.

When the subject of our first date comes up Sally always remembers that it was the same evening that the Beatles premiered on American TV—the Ed Sullivan Show. (She had a crush on George.) I, on the other hand, always recall her mother staring me down on her front porch. Sally was 19 and I was 20 when we met. Five years later we married.

There was a moment of awakening at Valley shortly before I received my A.A. degree. I had been there more than three years. My education began there. But I had also spent a lot of time goofing off with my fraternity brothers and in the poolroom, and got only middling grades.

The moment occurred outside the Theater Arts building, where I had encountered Aristotle. I stood on a slight rise surveying the campus. I reflected on my years at Valley and had this thought: *Richard, it's time to get on with adulthood.* This was novel—a notion I had never really entertained before. If it is possible to grow up some in an instant, it happened then and there.

In 2013 the CFA Institute presented me with its C. Stewart Sheppard Award in recognition of my contribution to the continuing education of its 150,000 members worldwide. The award included a sizable grant to the "institution of higher education" of my choice. Whoever dreamed up this award would not have anticipated the Sheppard endowment ever going to the likes of Valley JC, but that is where it went—the only school that would have me when I really needed a way to go.

After Valley I completed undergraduate studies at California State University at Northridge, also located in the San Fernando Valley. I did it in record time. I had matured some and gained purchase on the academic track. I was a regular on the dean's list. I was a business major with a concentration in finance. In those days it was largely the prosaic *descriptive* finance, rather than the *analytical* or *normative* types that were just beginning to be taught in leading business schools. But it was a start, at least. I did absorb the rudiments of present-value and cost-of-capital calculations.

PUTTING IT OUT AND GETTING IT BACK

During the two years of my upper-division studies at Northridge I worked for Pacific Finance, a consumer loan company. In those days finance company offices were commonplace. This is where working people financed automobile and furniture purchases and borrowed money at very high rates, often secured by a chattel mortgage on their furniture.

We spent half our time making and administering loans. We spent the other half trying to collect on those loans. In the industry, the business was known as "putting it out and getting back." There was no glamour whatsoever.

Prospective borrowers came to the office without an appointment. We sat them down in a hard booth with little privacy. We completed a credit app. In the upper right corner were untitled boxes simply numbered 1-4. We were to check one of the boxes. "1" meant White, "2" Black, "3" Mexican and "4" was Other. In the credit scoring system the "1's" got plus points and "2's" had points deducted. It was all very matter of fact.

Collecting the money was more interesting than lending it. When someone missed a payment we would call to remind them and get a payment date from them. If they were hard to reach at home, or we needed to get in their face a little, we would call them at work. At times we would ask them to come in for a consultation.

The work drew us into intimate aspects of the customers' lives. When telephoning failed to bring the money in, we went to their homes to collect, an activity known as "chasing." We wanted to know why they were having trouble staying current. We learned all about the circumstances of layoffs, domestic disputes and cars that had broken down. We figured out who were the alcoholics and who was unlucky.

One evening I sat on a thatched palm mat in the small, sparsely-furnished apartment of a huge young Samoan. He was naked save for the lava-lava he wore at home with his wife and small child. He was a gentle man, and I came to understand the sadness of his life here.

The last resort in collecting was repossession. A few incidents stuck with me. One woman, who had a good job, nice apartment and a Mexican housekeeper one day a week, simply could not stay current with the payments on her big color TV. I took another fellow in the office out to her apartment on a day I knew the housekeeper would be there. We knocked at the door and asked for the lady of the house, who we knew was at work. The housekeeper spoke no English, which I knew, having telephoned there several times. In Spanish I informed her that the *Señora* had called our television repair shop to have the set picked up and fixed. The housekeeper cordially showed us in. She and I exchanged pleasantries while we disconnected the TV and carted it out. *Adiós*. When the outraged woman called the office I told her to come in and pay off the loan and she could have her set back. Simple.

When seizing furniture with a warrant, we would be accompanied by a uniformed marshal as well as the auction house van. At first I thought having a guy with a gun on hand was overkill. After an encounter with a very large, very angry man I decided otherwise. I learned that there can be no greater humiliation than having people come into your home on a High Jewish Holiday and remove your belongings in front of your family. *Not* so simple.

What an education consumer finance proved to be. My time there was a hugely important part of my development.

In mid-1968 I completed my bachelor's degree and moved on from Cal State Northridge and from Pacific Finance, as well. In the fall I began graduate school at UCLA.

TWO

Discovering Finance Theory

Nobel laureate Harry Markowitz taught me portfolio theory. It was a first for both of us, although I readily concede he had a better grasp of the subject matter than I did. His seminal article on the subject had appeared 17 years earlier and his textbook 10 years earlier, but he had never taught the subject in a classroom.

I was taking the course as part of the M.B.A. curriculum at UCLA's Anderson School of Management in 1969. About half the people in the lecture hall were doing the same thing. The other half were graduate students and members of the faculty from a variety of disciplines from around the university plus a few eggheads from the RAND Corporation, the nearby think tank where Markowitz had once worked. Even then, long before he won the Nobel Prize in Economics for his portfolio selection theory, Markowitz was highly regarded for his work in matrix methods and simulation language programming.

Soon the students in Markowitz's class began separating into two groups. We M.B.A. students, who were getting our curriculum-tickets punched, so to speak, drifted to one side of the lecture hall. The scholars drifted to the other.

The divide was not lost on Professor Markowitz. He would begin each class addressing the M.B.A. students. He might draw cartoon-like, multi-tiered wheels of fortune on the board to explain jointly-distributed random variables. He spoke to us in a considerate voice, sounding more like Mr. Rogers than a professor.

As the lecture moved on, he began to address the academics directly. He might be discussing, say, the role of Lagrangian multipliers in computing efficient frontiers or waving his arms in the air to make a point in n-dimensional space. The words became unintelligible to our side of the room, but he continued in the same soothing Mr. Rogers voice. He was the picture of intellectual kindness to all.

When he shifted gears like this, some of the M.B.A. students would quietly close their notebooks and remove copies of the *Wall Street Journal* or *Barron's* from their briefcases. At the same time the other half would *open* their notebooks and begin to take notes.

I followed the lectures as best I could and pored over Markowitz's book. His portfolio theory was very different from the descriptive finance training I had had up to that point. It was my introduction to the concept of economic efficiency in portfolio design, a topic that would be central to my work in later years.

Portfolio theory à la Markowitz was unknown outside the university in those days. The computer code was not easily accessible and the computational requirements were too great for existing commercial processors. For these reasons the theory had languished in the academy for 17 years and would continue to do so for a few more.

In later years, when technological advances permitted widespread use of Markowitz's quadratic optimization methodology, I spent many hours using it in analyzing portfolios. For various reasons, some of which are discussed in an appendix, the methodology proved to have limited value in my work with clients. But it was a wonderful way to understand shifts in portfolio composition caused by even minor changes in assumptions. And my brief opportunity to learn from the master himself was an auspicious introduction to finance theory.

William Sharpe visited Westwood to deliver a lecture to the finance faculty and graduate students. He earned his doctorate at UCLA and had returned to discuss work that followed his seminal capital-asset-pricing theory. The lecture was purely theoretical.

When he concluded someone asked how the theory held up with data. Bill shuffled his feet a little. Then he replied in his characteristic retiring-but-self-confident manner. He said that he no longer bothered with data, implying that it just got in the way of important work. I loved the moment: the brilliant young scholar, quietly confident in his element.

Within a few short years Bill and I would meet again. The second encounter would begin a long-running association to bridge the divide between academy and practice that continues today. Bill helped me work through a finance-theory issue in a later section of this book.

I got a taste of analytical and normative finance at UCLA, thanks to the faculty and visiting scholars. I was taken with the idea of understanding investments in a *profound* way. My interest would continue well beyond graduate school. I realized I was a curious fellow, absorbed with questions such as, *What's going on here? How does this work? What's the larger context, the big picture? What makes economic sense? What has merit and what is folly?* An appreciation of finance theory helped me get at the answers. It would be important in my work to understand risk, asset-pricing and the many forms of economic friction and inefficiency attendant in investment.

THREE

A Foot in the Door

THE GO-GO YEARS OF FUND MANAGEMENT

About the time I started graduate school I got my first job in investments with Transamerica Fund Management Company in Los Angeles. This was the mutual fund management subsidiary of Transamerica Corporation. (Pacific Finance was also a Transamerica subsidiary. Some Pacific Finance executives who knew of my work at PF were kind enough to put in a good word for me with Transamerica's investment people, which is how I snagged the job with the mutual fund company.)

A man by the name of James Ledbetter hired me to work part-time. I worked two days a week in a kind of internship. My job was to write up—for the benefit of the funds' board of directors—companies whose shares he had recently added to one of the funds. This was a terrific starter job in investments for a graduate student.

Jim Ledbetter was what was known as a *gunslinger* in those days. He was a prime player in the red-hot stock market and a savvy buyer of the infamous story stocks of that era. In the late 1960s a lot of money managers believed that they should be routinely earning

15% a year in the stock market. Some did actual research. Others listened to the stories of oracles (usually brokers) about companies with fabulous prospects. For sure this was an era of aggressive money management.

I arrived early in the reception area of the mutual fund management company on the day I started the new job. The offices were on the 27th floor of the Occidental Life Tower in downtown Los Angeles. When Ledbetter arrived he was surprised to see me. He remembered who I was but that was about it. He had forgotten I was starting work that day and had nothing for me to do.

We walked down the hallway to his office. There he looked at his calendar. He saw that he was scheduled to attend a meeting later that morning at the offices of investment bankers in Beverly Hills. He had circled (tentatively agreed to purchase) one million dollars' worth of letter stock in a little-known technology company, subject to a personal meeting with the CEO. (Letter stock shares were unregistered, which meant that the investment was illiquid for a period of years.) Ledbetter was to meet with the CEO and investment bankers so that he could grill them before making a final commitment. He said casually in his soft Georgia drawl, "Richard, why don't you go on out there and handle that meeting. Let me know what you think of the opportunity."

I had about an hour to prepare before hopping in my car and heading for Beverly Hills. I found the offering prospectus and read it quickly. I read about the lines of business the company was in and their highly uncertain prospects. (This was a story stock, to be sure.) I reviewed their financial statements. I came up with some questions to ask at the meeting. Mr. Ledbetter's secretary, Pat, who would type term papers for me in a pinch, called the men I would be meeting with to let them know I would be there in Mr.

Ledbetter's stead. She scribbled their names on a piece of paper and handed it to me as I dashed out the door.

As I drove to the meeting I had but one thought. *Are you kidding me? Can this really be happening?* At the time I had a newly-minted bachelor's degree in finance from a local state college. The closest work experience I had had up to that point was making $300 loans to factory workers at Pacific Finance.

I arrived at the bankers' discreetly-lit, deep-carpeted and wood-paneled offices on a quiet Beverly Hills street. I was ushered into a conference room and offered coffee in a fine china cup and saucer. The gentlemen I met with were cordial and treated me with respect. I asked my questions, which led to a more general discussion of the business and its prospects.

I left them and returned to the office where I sat down and wrote a report for Mr. Ledbetter. A day or two later I got up the gumption to ask him if he had had a chance to read the report. He had, he said, and had gone ahead with the deal—all very matter of fact.

Another time I was to write up a company by the name of Parvin-Dohrmann for the board of directors. It was acquiring gambling interests in Las Vegas and showing rapidly-growing earnings. A whiff of ties to organized crime made the story tantalizing. We had nothing in writing on the company. Mr. Ledbetter gave me the name of the broker who had put him on to the stock and suggested I call him for information.

I called the gentleman, introduced myself and explained we were looking for factual information, financial statements, that sort of thing, on Parvin-Dohrmann. Over the din of brokerage house clamor, he yelled into the receiver, "You want information? I'll give you information. BUY! BUY! BUY!" and slammed the receiver down. I don't recall how I got the dope on Parvin-Dohrmann for my report. But I wasn't all that surprised by the incident. That's the way things were in the days of the story stocks.

Working with Jim Ledbetter and the bright young men he had with him, I learned a lot about the aggressive money management of the 1960s. One of my young colleagues there played the January Effect long before the academics got on to it. During the month of December he identified all the little companies in the Pink Sheets that had plummeted in value during the year. Late in the month he bought shares in ones still trading. In January he sold them for big profits.

My brief time with Jim Ledbetter launched my career in investments at a historic time. In addition to the knowledge I picked up, my year with him helped me gain self-confidence that would prove invaluable in later phases of my career.

A STINT WITH UNCLE SAM

While in graduate school at UCLA I was also a second lieutenant in the California Army National Guard. The Vietnam War was underway. Like a lot of young men I opposed the war and did not want to be drafted to fight it. Plus I had a lot going on in civilian life. And yet I felt I was as much of a patriot as the next guy. It was a conundrum shared by many. I resolved it by joining the National Guard. I selected an option that would provide officer training leading to a U.S. Army commission, and I deliberately opted for the infantry. Thus the dilemma became a coin toss: Heads, I would remain a civilian and receive excellent military training that accommodated my continued schooling. Tails, I would go to war as a soldier's soldier.

When I completed my M.B.A. studies I was scheduled to report to the U.S. Army Infantry School at Fort Benning, Georgia. I had already gone through basic training at Ft. Ord at Monterey Bay and attended officer candidate school at the California Military Academy at Camp San Luis Obispo. Now, as a second lieutenant, I was off to the infantry officers basic course to become a fully-trained platoon leader.

I would be at Ft. Benning for eight weeks. The *most interesting* experience there was forward observer (FO) training. I peered through binoculars and directed artillery fire at targets a mile away. Here I learned the technique known as *bracketing*. If the first round lands long by what you estimate to be 300 meters, by radio you direct the firing battery to "drop" 450 meters in aiming the next round. If the second round falls short by 150 meters, you know that your read of the range is correct. You then command, "Add 150 and fire for effect." (*Let 'em have it.*) The beauty of bracketing is that it reduces the potential for "creeping" toward the target in the event your perspective is misleading. I would frequently use bracketing as a simple search routine in my professional work.

The *hairiest* part of the infantry school experience was night patrol with the Rangers. I was impressed by the Rangers' brand of soldiering. One would appear seemingly out of nowhere to lead a group of lieutenants on a tactical nighttime patrol. Without saying a word he would head for the jungly terrain where we would spend the night. A dozen or so of us would follow, single file. The only thing you could see was the small fluorescent patch glued to the back of the soft cap of the man ten yards ahead of you. No one spoke or made a sound. In this fashion we moved over pitch-dark, steamy, swampy ground that the cottonmouths and alligators thought belonged to them. Shortly before dawn we found ourselves exiting the "jungle" at the same point we had entered. And without a word the Ranger walked off, seemingly to nowhere, never having spoken a word.

The *best* part of my posting at Ft. Benning was drinks and a steak dinner in the festive atmosphere of the officers club.

I got a bit gung-ho at Benning. I was tempted to extend my stay to attend Airborne School. I also entertained the idea of returning for Ranger training. But wife and life awaited me in Los Angeles. (My infantry regiment remained on standby for activation, though things never came to that for us. When my six years of service were up, I resigned my commission.)

I had arranged for a business school classmate, Bob Bartshe, to hold down my part-time job at Transamerica during my eight weeks at Ft. Benning so that I might have something to return to, i.e., a leg up in finding a full-time position in investments.

During my stint at Benning I received a letter from Bob. He described being called into the baronial office of Transamerica's supreme investment executive, George D. Bjurman, and summarily terminated. (Bjurman, a respected devotee of the Nifty-Fifty school of investing, soon thereafter would found his own investment firm in Century City.) Bjurman told Bob that Ledbetter-the-gunslinger had quit to join the recently-formed, razzle-dazzle firm of Cogan, Berlin, Weill & Levitt in New York, where his style was a better fit than at stodgy Transamerica. Bjurman said they were reorganizing the operation along more conventional lines and had eliminated our position. According to Bob, Bjurman said, "So, Richard [sic], we have to let you go."

My friend Bob loved the job and was only too happy to throw me under the bus. Recognizing the old boy was a bit confused, Bob said, deftly, "Oh, but you see, Mr. Bjurman, I'm not Richard Ennis. Ennis is on military leave. I'm Bob Bartshe." Bjurman, unfazed, said, "I see. You are...Bartshe, not Ennis. Alright, Bartshe, *you* are fired. And if you hear from Ennis, please advise him *he* is fired, too."

For years Bob, with whom I remained good friends and who also entered the Los Angeles investment community after UCLA, delighted in recounting over drinks how he had been fired twice in one day—first as me and then as himself.

For my part I had the presence of mind to proceed as if I knew nothing of the events back in Los Angeles. I wrote to Bjurman on Ft. Benning stationery. I told him how grand it was doing my patriotic duty but that I was ready to return to meet with him to discuss my future at Transamerica. It worked. He granted me an interview upon my return.

The interview took place a few weeks later and included the head of Transamerica Investment Management Company, Inc., a sister subsidiary of the mutual fund management company. This subsidiary handled separate investment accounts of wealthy families and institutions and was actively recruiting at the time. I hit it off with the Transamerica executives, and they offered me a full-time position as a securities analyst. I had played my cards well enough and Lady Luck smiled on me. As things turned out, she kept an eye on me throughout my career.

FOUR

Money Management

SECURITIES ANALYSIS AND PORTFOLIO MANAGEMENT

t Transamerica Investment Management I began researching stocks that the portfolio managers might add to the clients' portfolios. It was 1970 and growth stocks were all the rage. This was the era of the Nifty Fifty high-quality growth companies: IBM, Xerox, Johnson & Johnson, Merck, Avon, McDonalds and so on. Perhaps the most telling label for these darlings was *one-decision* stocks. The notion was that these companies were so wondrous they could and would *grow* their way through anything. Valuation? Irrelevant. These trees grew to the sky. It was the ethos of the times. These stocks made up more than half of Transamerica's client portfolios. Even when filling in behind them, the emphasis was on growth. The S&L's were considered a growth play. Even in the utility sector, the bias was toward companies in growth markets. Valuation would not raise its ugly head until the great bear market of 1973-74.

There was nothing to be done with the first tier of growth stocks apart from admiring them and owning them. So I concentrated my research on second-tier growth stocks. Most of my recommendations proved to be winners. I was beginning to earn my chops as a stock picker.

I began the CFA program at Transamerica when the program was still in its early days. Senior members of our firm had been grandfathered in among the first CFAs. I took the three exams and was awarded Charter 3638.

As I became familiar with the management company's operation I observed that it employed an antiquated, manual portfolio accounting system. I volunteered to undertake a major project to automate the entire process, although the extent of my computer knowledge was limited to a single class in FORTRAN in grad school. I located and contracted with a bright group of young men from the University of Chicago who ran a software firm in Hinsdale, Illinois, called Catallactics Corporation. Together we designed and implemented a state-of-the-art portfolio accounting and analytics system for the company. I was developing a reputation as being something of a whiz kid at Transamerica.

The senior executives began to introduce me to clients. The investment business was changing, and youth played well at the time. I moved right along and was made Vice President. At the age of 27 I was proposed to manage the money of Hills Bros. Coffee in San Francisco, one of that city's venerable businesses. Transamerica itself is a San Francisco institution. Established by A.P. Giannini, it was the holding company for his diverse interests, including Bank of America, which he had founded at the turn of the century.

Hills Bros. Coffee was also founded at the turn of the century. (You can forget the Boston Brahmins and the old families of New

York and Philadelphia; no aristocrat is more self-aware than the old-line San Franciscan.) The Hills Bros.' offices were still in the Romanesque revival building on the Embarcadero that is now a landmark. A senior Transamerica executive and I visited there so that members of the family could meet me, their would-be investment manager.

We were welcomed by two gentlemen in the executive offices. It turned out that these fellows were the reigning Hills brothers (or cousins, I'm not sure which) who ran the company. They shared a plain office—pale green paint on plaster walls—with a high ceiling and worked at their great grandfathers' roll-top desks.

They were polite, unassuming men. We took a seat and the interview began. This was our chance to persuade them that a fellow two years out of business school—and that would be UCLA, not Stanford—from Los Angeles, no less, could be trusted to handle their money. It was a make-or-break opportunity if there ever was one.

"Tell us about yourself, Richard," one of them said. So I did.

"Well, I can tell you I'm the right man to manage your money, gentlemen. You see, I was *born* here—across town at Children's Hospital. My parents lived in the Marina.

"Hills Bros. was the only coffee my mother would have in the house. She drank it strong and black; I was practically weaned on the stuff.

"*And*, my uncle was an executive in your New Jersey operation."

"Your uncle—really? What was his name?" one asked.

"Fred Byers."

They both lit up. "Why, Fred was practically a member of the family...."

I don't recall what was said after that. It really didn't matter. My career as an institutional investment manager—and salesman—had been launched. Sometimes things just break your way.

BLOCK TRADER

I spent a memorable week manning Transamerica's trading desk while our trader was on vacation. We had just decided to liquidate our substantial holdings of utility stocks, so there would be plenty of work to do.

I quickly discovered that Bear Stearns, one of the top block-trading firms on Wall Street, had one or more large buyers and was able to move our positions fairly easily, with many trades occurring on upticks. By Friday of that week I was down to one holding, 92,500 shares of Potomac Electric. This was a huge position in view of the stock's meager average daily trading volume. The stock had been trading several hundred shares a day at 15¼–⅜. I showed Bear the position and they began to salivate. They quickly put together a bid for the entire position at 15. I was feeling pretty good about my week's work and was reluctant to let the last utility shares go on a down-tick. So I declined the bid.

Half an hour later the Bear line lit up and I answered. "Hey Dick! Cy Lewis here. Our guys tell me you need help getting rid of your Potomac Electric." Salim ("Cy" to everyone on Wall Street) Lewis was Bear Stearns's managing partner and legendary head trader. Cy Lewis, along with Gus Levy of Goldman Sachs, had pioneered block trading on Wall Street. And in the next few hours he instructed me in some of the fine points.

Lewis told me the situation "down there" on the floor of the New York Stock Exchange was deteriorating for electric utilities. Nevertheless, he was prepared to make a *better* offer than I had gotten earlier. He would take the entire position off my hands at 15 a share. I hit my Quotron. It looked like POM had stopped trading, the last being at 15 ¼. I said, "But Mr. Lewis, that's the same price your guys offered me earlier."

"Yeah, it is. But given what's happening, it's a much *better* price now than it was then." I declined, thanked him for his personal interest and put the receiver down.

He called an hour later with the same pitch, only things had gotten even more dire "down there." He offered me the same price, telling me it was better yet considering the circumstances. "No thanks," I said. But I was getting nervous. I was long a ton of a thinly-traded stock that I had instructions to sell, a stock whose shares had stopped trading. And I had a reasonable offer in hand.

Before the close the Bear line lit up again. "Dick, you are really one tough son of a gun. I discussed this trade with my partners over a martini at lunch. We need your stock. I am now prepared to offer you a truly fantastic price."

"15?" I asked.

"Yeah, it's a real bloodbath down there, Dick."

"I'll take it," I said.

A minute or two later I saw my print: 92,500 POM 15. After another few minutes I noticed trading resume—200 shares at 15 ¼ and, just before the close, 300 at 15 ⅜. Trading in Potomac Electric had returned to normal.

In his *Times* obituary Cy Lewis was described by a colleague as "the greatest telephone salesman in the business." You would get no argument from me.

THE GOOD LIFE

Sally and I were in the fast lane during my three years managing money for Transamerica. We were wined and dined by institutional stockbrokers, coming to know all the finest restaurants in town. We enjoyed good seats at Laker games, gratis, of course, as well as tickets to the Indy-style open-wheel Inaugural at the Ontario Motor Speedway. All this and more was owing to the munificence of the stockbrokers. The brokers, of course, were lubricated by the commissions generated by our clients' portfolios, and this was before negotiated rates.

On one memorable occasion we were entertained by a prominent broker, Bob Brandt, at his Beverly Hills mansion. We arrived for dinner and the screening of a movie that had just been released in the theaters. We were greeted at the front door by Bob's glamorous wife. "Hi, I'm Janet!" Once inside Sally pulled me aside and asked me if I knew who Bob's wife was.

"Janet," I said.

"That's not what I mean, dummy. She's Janet *Leigh*, the famous actress."

We had a pleasant evening with Bob and Janet at their palatial home, after which we returned to our $150-a-month apartment in the Valley like a couple of Cinderellas.

RESTLESSNESS

During those early years of managing money I realized my training in the field of finance was already becoming dated. In the late 1960s and early 1970s the efficient market, or random walk, theory was beginning to be noted by progressive investment people. The gist of the theory is that stock prices reflect all available information.

Price fluctuations, therefore, would be random (unpredictable), because news, by its nature, enters the market unpredictably. The implication of this is that no one can beat the market. An implication for *me* was that while I might earn a handsome living in my current line of work, there was a question about its *meaning*.

Sitting in my office one day I undertook a thought experiment. I imagined that I drove a cement truck for a living. Assuming I made four trips a day on average from the yard to a construction site, I could estimate the number of trips I would make in a year. With a little more information I could estimate my contribution to Gross National Product for the year. Thus, I could determine my economic value, which would always be a positive figure, however small. But what if I was just shuffling stocks around in clients' portfolios without adding to the return of a stock market index? The index fund wouldn't appear on the scene for a few more years, but the implications were clear nonetheless. The niggling question of meaning persisted.

While ruminating on my career I came in contact with two fellows who were among the earliest proponents of academic investment concepts that were filtering into the commercial realm. John O'Brien was one, Dennis Tito the other. They introduced me to what would become the analytics of the new school. They were promoting this technology for a brokerage firm, Jas. Oliphant & Co.

They calculated beta coefficients for individual stocks and were the first ones to do so in a commercial setting. (Common stock betas are factors that indicate price volatility relative to the market.) They had rudimentary software to enable a client to calculate the cross-sectional, or point-in-time, beta for a stock portfolio. This could be used to determine a portfolio's risk-adjusted performance.

In 1970 this was the cutting edge. On behalf of Transamerica I subscribed to their service and began introducing my colleagues to what was known then as *modern capital theory* (and later as MPT, for modern portfolio theory).

This was the beginning of a new era. Investment managers could observe the level of their portfolios' market-relative risk and degree of diversification. As a result, they began to understand what—apart from their sheer brilliance—might account for the returns earned by their portfolios.

The California Institute of Technology in Pasadena was a client of Transamerica. Colleagues asked me to attend an investment committee meeting to discuss the ramifications of modern capital theory. We surmised Caltech would be a logical place to introduce what was then truly an academic idea.

At the meeting I made a very basic presentation of how return and risk are related using a simple scatter plot. It emphasized that an investor's risk posture was a matter of choice and taste. Harold Brown had recently left his position as Secretary of the Air Force and been named president of Caltech. Having earned his Ph.D. in physics from Columbia University at the age of 21, Brown was quick to pick up on the implication of our simple presentation. When we concluded, he said to the committee, "Gentlemen, Mr. Ennis is telling us we have a decision to make." I thought, *Now this is the type of dialogue an investment advisor should be having with his clients.*

FIVE
Early Days of Quant Investing

LEAP OF FAITH

Before long, O'Brien and Tito had a falling out with Oliphant, to which they were attracting a large, lucrative stream of commissions from giant New York banks eager not to be left out of what might become a big thing (which it did). So they formed O'Brien Associates to carry on the business. John and Dennis had fine credentials in engineering and economics. John was the roving evangelist, while geeky Dennis, back in the office, cooked up the beta coefficients that were now selling like hotcakes. After establishing themselves they asked me to join the firm to help spread the word, especially with institutional investors, such as corporate pension funds and university endowments.

Joining this fledgling effort would be a huge career decision. I was on a great track at Transamerica. But managing money did not appear as though it would satisfy my appetite for work that I found meaningful and which would channel my creative and intellectual energies. I was sorely tempted to join O'Brien Associates.

Sally was supportive of the move. So in 1972, at the age of 28, I bade farewell to money management and the city's leading *maître d's*. I began commuting to the foot of Wilshire Boulevard in Santa Monica to offices perched on the palisades overlooking the Pacific Ocean.

NOTEWORTHIES

O'Brien Associates was never more than a very small firm. Yet, situated at the ocean's edge, it proved to be a veritable tidal pool of latent talent in the early days of the modern way. Most of these people became prominent in their own right in the years ahead.

John W. O'Brien did more than anyone I can think of to introduce modern capital theory to the investment profession. In 1970 he began to crisscross the country, explaining Sharpe's capital asset pricing model (CAPM) to investment management organizations, few of which had ever really been exposed to it. He dissected investment managers' beta coefficients to help them understand the difference between relative risk and correlation. He explained diversification in measurable terms. He was a born teacher.

About 10 years later he developed an abiding interest in managing risk *over time* and became a pioneer in financial engineering, as well. Like many of us, he thought that the relationship of the value of one's assets to the value of one's liabilities should play a role in determining investment policy. A logical extension of this proposition is that rational investors should *revise* their asset allocation as the value of assets and liabilities fluctuate over time. This led John to form the asset management firm Leland O'Brien Rubinstein Associates (LOR) with Hayne Leland and Mark Rubinstein of UC Berkeley to manage portfolios using dynamic hedging. The underlying finance principle was options-pricing theory. They were quite successful in gathering assets, but not for the precise purpose they imagined. Their clients, rather than subscribing to the elegant logic of dynamic asset allocation, wanted *portfolio insurance*. They wanted LOR to create "protective puts" on their stock holdings during a queasy stock market period. The thunderous crash of 1987 revealed flaws in the state of the art that would bring about a reassessment of portfolio insurance. Critics claimed that portfolio insurance trading exacerbated the steep market decline. John O'Brien, nevertheless stands as a towering figure in the advancement of modern capital theory and financial engineering.

John is Professor Emeritus of Financial Engineering, Haas School of Business, UC Berkeley, and co-founder of its Master of Financial Engineering program. He was a prime mentor of mine and remains a dear friend.

Dennis Tito's surpassing interest was as a businessman. This would become evident in the success of the firm he would subsequently build, Wilshire Associates. He would become a wealthy man, at one point paying a tidy sum to be the first tourist in outer space.

Gilbert Beebower became a highly regarded industry intellectual. He was a graduate of Caltech and worked in scientific engineering out of school. With John O'Brien he was a pioneer of modern capital theory in the institutional investment community. He became a one-man think tank for SEI Investments, and consulted with stock exchanges around the world. He was a member of the Brady Commission. He consulted for the U.S. Department of Labor and the Securities and Exchange Commission. Always a gentleman, Gil was awarded the Matthew R. MacArthur award as an industry leader in 2013, the year he passed away.

David Booth, a former student of Eugene Fama at the University of Chicago, joined the firm from Wells Fargo Bank, where he had been involved in efforts to launch one the earliest S&P 500 index funds, known as the Stagecoach Fund. David would ultimately achieve fame and fortune with his brainchild, Dimensional Fund Advisors. I recall his sharing with me in 1980 a paper by Rolf Banz that demonstrated the extraordinary returns achieved by small company stocks. And then David went and did it for real by founding Dimensional. The University of Chicago renamed its Business School the Booth School in his honor. David has remained a steadfast friend since those early days.

Wayne Wagner and Larry Cuneo were part of the crew, also joining from Wells Fargo. Wayne would gain notoriety as a leading authority in understanding and measuring transaction costs in stock trading. He has published on that subject and an array of others in leading journals and books. His research has won many awards. In 1986 Wayne and Larry would found Plexus Group, which became the preeminent provider of transaction cost consulting and measurement services.

Gifford Fong left O'Brien Associates to found his eponymous consulting firm specializing in quantitative analysis of fixed income securities. Gifford has published extensively in leading journals. He edited *Financial Analysts Journal* for a number of years before Rob Arnott and then I did. He is the author of several books and editor of several collections. His firm has been a respected advisor in quantitative investment for more than four decades.

The overriding interest of yours truly was working with the principal decision makers for an investment portfolio to establish investment policy in its proper context. More narrowly, my work would focus on achieving economic efficiency in the management of institutional investment portfolios. Recurring themes were risk control and cost control. If you incur risk, you should get paid. Expenditures should result in tangible benefit.

It took a few months at O'Brien Associates for it to sink in that I was a salesman. I needed to pick up the telephone and cold-call financial executives of major corporations and college and university treasurers. I needed to explain briefly why it was in their interest to meet with me to learn how esoteric financial concepts might benefit them. And I needed a traveling bag because most of the prospects were east of the Mississippi River.

INNOVATION

So, what did all the hotshots at O'Brien Associates actually *do*? I mentioned that the firm provided tapes of beta coefficients of individual stocks to the largest investment firms, which were primarily Eastern banks in those days. We taught them capital market theory and how to do risk-adjusted performance measurement. Our team also began to introduce these techniques to pension plan sponsors. It is difficult to describe what a watershed this was in the practice of investment management; it was a truly transformative period in its history.

We introduced one of the first, if not the first, commercial mean-variance optimization models. Dennis had walked down Ocean Avenue to the nearby RAND Corporation and picked up at a nominal cost a document titled QP4. This was, in essence, Markowitz's code. Although people understood the concept of quadratic optimization with linear constraints, owing to its computational complexity and the prevailing state of computer processing, no practitioners had really worked with portfolio optimization. Our optimizer made it possible to do so. Nowadays, analysts in every consulting firm can bang out a boatload of optimizations in an afternoon using Excel's Solver function.

O'Brien Associates innovated pension investment modeling in connection with work for a man by the name of George Williams who was Treasurer of Illinois Bell Telephone Company in Chicago. George was one of the first executives on the pension plan sponsor side to embrace modern capital theory. This was the very first instance of conducting what is widely-known today as asset-liability modeling, or simply ALM.

Working with Illinois Bell's actuaries, the O'Brien team forecast pension plan liabilities many years into the future. (Actuaries project plan benefit payments out approximately 50 years and then use present-value discounting to estimate the pension plan's *liability*. Our approach necessitated projecting the liability itself 20 years into the future.)

Once the liability projection was done, we reproduced the actuary's funding method, which is the algorithm by which the actuary determines each year's required contribution to the plan based on observed asset and liability values.

On the asset side we employed Monte Carlo simulation methods to model investment uncertainty. This enabled us to create probability distributions for key financial parameters, such as future levels of corporate contributions and the plan's funded status under alternative stock-bond policies. This enabled us to map otherwise nebulous investment risk (i.e., standard deviation of return) into familiar, concrete financial terms for the decision makers.

O'Brien Associates also conducted early research into the operation of the stock index fund. One of the issues then was whether to replicate the index—own all 500 names in the S&P 500—or to sample them; there is a trade-off between transaction cost and tracking error. As we know now, replication won out.

O'Brien Associates created the first total stock market index, which included approximately 5,000 names. *The Wall Street Journal* publishes it daily as the Total Stock Market Index. A Vanguard mutual fund of that name is available to everyday investors at a cost of four basis points.

These were heady times for quant pioneers.

GATEWAY TO THE (ACADEMIC) STARS

Given the nature of the talent and the type of work we were doing, it is no surprise that we came in contact with finance academics. These included Bill Sharpe at Stanford, Fischer Black, then at the University of Chicago, Jim Lorie and Myron Scholes of Chicago and Peter Williamson of Dartmouth College's Amos Tuck School. I developed enduring collaborations and friendships with Bill and Fischer, in particular. In the years ahead, these and other academics would become an important part of my professional circle. They provided my flesh-and-blood connection to finance theory.

EARLY DEMISE

Everything went along well enough until O'Brien and Tito had a falling out. When the reason for the breach came to light, I concluded that I could not be in business with Mr. Tito. The abrupt end to O'Brien Associates threw a monkey wrench into the careers of a lot of talented people.

Tito would build Wilshire Associates from what was left of the firm, rising like a Phoenix from the ashes.

John O'Brien had been courted by the Chicago firm of A.G. Becker & Co. for some time. John, Gil Beebower, David Booth and

I opted to join Becker to infuse their large, national fund-performance-measurement business with the most modern technology. I went along with considerable trepidation given the circumstances. This turn of events, however, proved serendipitous.

I would have an office in Century City but my work was in Chicago. I became a cross-country commuter with a second residence at the Union League Club of Chicago beginning in the spring of 1975. I was 31 at the time. My young family would move to Evanston later that year. Our first son, John, was two when we embarked on the road trip to the Middle West in our Volvo sedan. We encountered heavy snow in Joplin, Missouri, and picked up tire chains for the rest of the drive. The Californians pressed on undaunted, arriving in Chicago on Thanksgiving Day in a swirling snowstorm.

SIX

The A.G. Becker Years: 1975-1980

BECKER'S ORIGINS

.G. Becker & Co., founded in 1893, was a *Chicago* firm in the same vein as Carl Sandburg's 1914 poem, *Chicago*, and Nelson Algren's 1951 essay, *City on the Make*.

Sandburg's *Chicago* opens with:

> Hog Butcher for the World,
> Tool Maker, Stacker of Wheat,
> Player with Railroads and the Nation's Freight Handler;
> Stormy, husky, brawling,
> City of the Big Shoulders...

Sandburg later described the poem as "...a chant of defiance by Chicago... its defiance of New York, Boston, Philadelphia, London, Paris, Berlin and Rome. The poem sort of says "Maybe we ain't got culture, but we're eatin' regular." [Note: Corwin, Norman. *The World of Carl Sandburg*. Harcourt, Brace & World. p. 32.]

The title of Algren's essay says it all: *a city on the make.*

The Becker I joined comprised a group of first-rate brokers and bankers, absent any airs. They hustled in a freewheeling but focused professional and ethical environment. Everyone was busy with their own bustling business, of which there were many. Profits abounded. Overhead was virtually nonexistent. Little was to be gained from politicking. At first I was flattered when they offered to make me a shareholder. Then I realized they were simply sponging up every last dab of capital to put it to work in deal-making and trading. They were benignly on the make among their own, so to speak. A.G. Becker was a wonderful, entrepreneurial place to be in those days.

THE BIRTH OF INVESTMENT CONSULTING

Becker is widely and rightly regarded as the birthplace of institutional investment consulting. The seeds were germinated in the early-1960s by a fellow named John Mabie, with whom I would later become friendly. John and some other brokers were looking for new sources of commission revenue. They knew that corporate clients did not have a clue how their pension and profit sharing funds were doing. The Becker brokers approached corporate treasurers with an offer they could not refuse. Becker would gather data from bank custodians, calculate a rate of return and report it back, comparing it with the returns of other funds. And it would not cost the company a penny. All they had to do was direct their fund manager to trade with Becker. Thus were born the ubiquitous percentile ranks of the performance-reporting industry.

Performance evaluation first took take shape as a line of business for Becker in 1965, when a few key players began to organize it as a formal part of the business. The Funds Evaluation Division, or FED, as it was known at Becker, was formally launched in 1967. Management began recruiting a sales force that over time would morph into a consultant force. They added product development, systems and production specialists as well as support personnel.

There was a real need for fund performance evaluation services in the marketplace and no real competition. FED created specialized versions of its performance report for various market segments—corporations and endowments as well as public and union funds. Another version of the report was offered to investment managers, who were eager to better understand the watchdog that was now overseeing their work. The sales force rolled on. Within the first six or seven years Becker acquired more than 1,000 clients, achieving a 70% market share for fund performance evaluation.

As the market matured, members of the sales force found themselves spending more time servicing accounts. The Becker rep was typically the only person meeting with clients to discuss investments apart from the fund managers themselves. The reps began to expand the type of consultation they provided. The clients welcomed the help and increasingly relied upon it.

There proved to be limitations to how much help the sales-consultant reps could provide for their clients. Noticeably absent were formalized approaches to establishing investment policy and assistance in selecting investment managers. Other firms were beginning to offer these as specialized services. Becker was well aware of this activity and realized it was both a threat and an opportunity. A chance to help seize that opportunity is what took me to Becker.

A PARTNERSHIP IS BORN

James F. Knupp and I were to work together to put A.G. Becker in the investment policy advisory business. Jim was an AGB veteran in the management of Funds Evaluation. He knew the performance-reporting business and all the sales-consultant reps through whom we would work in the marketplace. I brought the finance expertise. We were a team. Jim proved to be a quick study and soon distinguished himself professionally as an expert in advising on investment policy. For the two of us it was the beginning of a partnership that would endure over many years through thick and thin.

Things were not always easy between us; we did not always see eye to eye. Jim's equable temperament would prove to be a useful counterbalance to my sometimes impetuous nature. We partnered, in other words.

We shared values—not least of which was the importance of courtesy and consideration in dealing with one another and others—that later on would inform the culture of EnnisKnupp and sustain our personal bond.

Jim and I also shared a talent, one that would prove invaluable to us as consultants and as a model for associates. Both of us had an instinct for proving ourselves indispensable to every client; we each did it in our own way. I have heard this referred to as super-pleasing by experts on the subject. To us it was simply a matter of making it impossible for a client to ever dump us.

Jim retired from EnnisKnupp in 1998, continuing as a member of the board of directors until the sale of the firm in 2010. In 2007 the Investment Management Consultants Association honored Jim and me with its Matthew R. MacArthur Award in recognition of our contribution to investment consulting. We remain good friends, enjoying breakfast together with some regularity as we often did in years gone by. Nowadays we agree on absolutely everything.

"I'LL HAVE TO CALL YOU BACK, SIR."

Not long after starting at Becker I was sitting in my new office at Clark and Madison Streets in Chicago's Loop. I picked up the telephone and dialed what was then known as the Investment Analysts Society of Chicago (now CFA Chicago Society). I told the woman that answered the phone that I wanted to apply for membership. (I was already a CFA and a member of Los Angeles Society by virtue of my position in money management with Transamerica.) She said, "Okay. But first I have to ask you a question. What line of work are you in?" We were not even sure what to call ourselves in those days. After a moment's reflection I said, "I guess you would call me a consultant."

There was a long pause. And then she said, "I'll have to call you back, sir. But I don't think the Society *takes* people like you." Well, I made it; and I have been a member of the Chicago CFA Society ever since. In fact, they honored me with their top (Friedman) award in 2016 for contributions to the profession.

That long-ago incident brought into relief a reality that the nascent field of investment consulting would have to face. Namely, conventional investment professionals were leery of us. We would have to prove ourselves and would spend many years doing it.

INVESTMENT POLICY AND MANAGER SEARCH

The first new service introduction at Becker was the pension modeling technique that O'Brien Associates folks had innovated with Illinois Bell Tel. (Now days this is known as asset-liability modeling, or ALM.) This meant mapping abstract risk (standard deviation of return) into familiar financial parameters for investment-policy decision-makers. We also employed the Monte Carlo simulation technique described earlier with college and university endowment funds. This enabled them, too, to appraise alternative stock-bond policies in concrete terms, such as the potential impact of those policies on future amounts of spending from endowment.

Now, for the first time, Becker was helping clients to actually establish investment policy. This meant Becker had become an investment *advisor* to institutional investors. This was a change for Becker, which had remained cautious about assuming an advisory role until it knew it was ready.

The second major offering was a service to evaluate investment management firms in order to make recommendations to clients as to which they might hire. This would come to be known as the manager search business, a staple of every modern investment consultant. We had to build a research department to accomplish this, which we did. Manager search was also a substantive advisory service for Becker.

The investment manager research work, by the way, brought me into contact with Jack Bogle. This happened when Becker was hired to find a new home for two Allstate Insurance Company mutual funds that wound up being merged into two Vanguard funds. This was long before Vanguard became a household name, and Jack was glad to have the business while he was building Vanguard.

In the course of the Allstate project Jack wrote the most compelling proposal I had ever seen. It stood out from the others we received. It spoke with clarity and not a bit of boilerplate or sales talk. It read more like an unembellished business plan than a solicitation. That proposal factored heavily into Vanguard's winning the business. The impression it made stuck with me and became the model of every proposal that would go out with my name or my firm's name on it.

Jack was a truly great man and, of course, a fellow champion of index fund investing. He would become a lifelong correspondent as well as a big supporter of EnnisKnupp in the years ahead.

After manager search came the development of additional consulting services for institutional investors. These would round out the service offerings of one of the first comprehensive institutional investment consulting entities anywhere.

Becker's Funds Evaluation sales-consultant force and clients were cautious in their embrace of our work at first. After about two years things picked up appreciably. After four years the consulting practice was flourishing, becoming the busiest of just a handful of those that were doing what we were doing.

AN IMPORTANT LESSON FROM A CLIENT

We built a state-of-the-art pension investment model for Eli Lilly and Company in Indianapolis. The folks there were very pleased with how the process gave context to their investment-policy decision-making. During the course of that project I reinforced the importance of having a sound investment policy and cautioned against over-reliance on active managers to ensure success.

A few months after we completed the project, Fred Ruebeck, who oversaw employee benefit fund investments for Lilly, called to tell me he wanted to hire us for manager search. I replied that I was a little surprised to hear it in light of my sobering words about active management during the course of our work together. Fred replied that the reason he wanted *our* help in selecting a manager was so that he would *have* a sober advisor.

There is a lesson here for investment consultants. The comparatively modest fees you collect for manager search work are testimony to the fact that neither client nor consultant has confidence in the latter's ability—or anyone else's, for that matter—to pick market-beating managers.

Consider an example: A client hires a consultant to select an active stock portfolio manager for a $25 million portfolio, agreeing to pay a search fee of $25,000. The compensation, in other words, is a *one-time* payment of 10 basis points of asset value. This level of compensation is not indicative of the promise of performance typified by hedge fund fees or other types of incentive compensation arrangements.

Clearly, neither client nor consultant has confidence in the consultant's ability to reliably pick a manager who can beat the market. So what is the client paying the consultant to do? The client needs the consultant's resources to help them do their job as a fiduciary. The client is buying professional services, not renting a Midas touch.

Consultant: You do not have to represent that you can pick managers that will beat the market. Try acknowledging the economic realities of the undertaking, namely, the existence of reasonably efficient markets and the cost of active management. Explain that your firm's manager research work is diligent and thorough. And here is the important part: Understand that clients, while hopeful about the potential of active investing, will value your candor.

PERSONAL PROGRESS

The Becker years were a great developmental period for me. First, I was getting a tremendous amount of experience with clients. In this respect it was like interning for air traffic control at O'Hare Field.

Second, I was using my knowledge to design and create investment consulting capabilities, some of which would become industry norms.

Third, I was becoming known more broadly in the institutional investment community. I had come to occupy a fairly high-profile position in the industry by virtue of what I was doing and how I was going about it.

Fourth, I was gaining experience in managing a busy consulting business.

All of these things would prove to be important to me before long.

HANDWRITING ON THE WALL

As our influence grew in the institutional investment community, inevitable conflicts of interest would arise within the large brokerage and investment banking firm of which we were a part.

One day the president of Becker, Jack Wing, asked me to his office to discuss a matter. It turned out that one of the firm's largest clients—one of every brokerage firm's largest clients—felt neglected by our manager research team. The chief investment officer of Morgan Guaranty (J.P. Morgan), the largest manager of institutional funds in the world then, had informed Jack that Morgan had suspended trading through Becker's desk and would welcome a visit by yours truly. Jack asked me if I might be good enough to speak with the gentleman. Hmm.

It became apparent that for our work helping clients select investment managers to be taken seriously it was vital that we be perceived as independent of the investment management community. We could not have managers paying us fees. Nor could we operate in an environment that was heavily reliant on staying in the good graces of money managers.

My father, John Ennis, and mother, Patricia Warren Ennis, steeped in Catholic moral teaching all her life, shaped my sense of right and wrong. It would not do to simply have the biggest or most influential investment consulting business in the land. It had to be done right.

As I looked around, there was no other firm I would have wanted to join. Most had conflicts of their own. None were doing work more interesting or relevant than ours. It became increasingly clear that, if I wanted to keep doing what I was doing in a truly independent, professional environment, I would have to hang out my own shingle somehow. This was not something I had ever envisioned doing. Nor was it good timing for me to get all entrepreneurial.

After a career as a certified shorthand (court) reporter, Sally was now at home with our twin baby boys, Colin and Ryan. John was six years old and starting school. And we were in the process of bringing my mother, dying of lung cancer and whom we supported financially, from California to live nearby. Such was the hand Sally was playing when I began lamenting my situation at work and raising the possibility of quitting a perfectly good job to pursue an idea, a mere concept.

In the fall of 1980 I floated the idea of breaking off from Becker with Jim Knupp and a few others. We had weekend discussions, some in my living room, others at the Glen View Club, where Jim was a member. Several people participated in the discussions at one point or another. I could see people were really enthusiastic about the idea of forming a different type of consulting business— more like a professional practice. My confidence grew. I wrote a business plan. Most importantly, Sally was supportive.

When all was said and done Jim Knupp and Ronald Gold would join me in establishing a new firm. Ron worked for me and led our investment manager research team. We three were the core of the Becker consulting unit and would launch our own firm.

HAPPY ENDING

When the time came to resign, Jim and I went to our manager and informed him of our decision. Seventy client projects were in the works at the time. We realized our departure would leave a big hole in the consulting activity and offered separation alternatives that would minimize disruption of the services being provided to clients. We offered to clear out that day, a not-uncommon practice in brokerage firms. Or we could give two weeks' notice. Or we could extend our employment for a period of several weeks in order to minimize the impact of our departure.

After giving it some thought, our manager proposed that we depart at our earliest convenience, set up shop and have the work in progress subcontracted to us for completion. This was an ideal solution. It was good for Becker and the clients, and it was great for us. We had not solicited any of the clients for obvious ethical reasons, and had no revenue prospects lined up when we went in to resign. The Becker work would provide substantial revenue from day one that would last for six months, long enough for us to make a start.

Hooray! More good fortune. Sally would *not* have to find a sitter and get back to court reporting after all.

Dorothy Gifford was my secretary at the time. (In those long ago days everyone referred to such workers as "secretaries.") A petite, gentle woman, perhaps 15 years my elder, she believed deeply that it was her mission in life to look after me. She insisted on joining the new effort, despite having a good salary, seniority and a nice profit sharing balance with Becker. She pointed out that we would need someone at the administrative level, which was true. "But Dorothy," I said, "you're set for life here. Besides, we don't have any clients lined up and not a whole lot of capital. Just between you and me, going into this thing we don't have a pot to you-know-what in." She replied, "Well, *I* have a pot." Dorothy knew how to close a deal. She was dear to me and worked for EnnisKnupp until her retirement many years later. We danced at her retirement party.

THE END OF BECKER

Warburg (London) and Paribas (Paris) bought stakes in Becker in 1974 and later acquired control. If they had been content to simply receive substantial year-end distributions, things might have worked out better. Alas, they sought "synergies" and influence in the running of Becker. What a disaster. The cultures of Continent and Chicago couldn't have been more at odds with one another. The Americans from the Middle West endured hours-long luncheons in private dining rooms in Paris and London. The European partners would have to put up with a box lunch on a conference room table in Chicago. Everything that could go wrong did. The Europeans' handpicked man to oversee Becker was a New York attorney without experience running a securities firm. His name was Ira Wender. Working with the steady support of the Europeans, Wender proved to be a one-man wrecking crew at Becker. As testimony to the sturdiness of A.G. Becker, it took the bungling Europeans and Wender 10 years to run it into the ground.

Funds Evaluation was sold to SEI Corporation in 1983 in the course of Becker's demise. Some employees joined the buyer, which soon morphed into a money manager. The event also triggered a diaspora of Becker Funds Evaluation folks to positions all over the investment landscape. The brother- and sisterhood of A.G. Becker's Funds Evaluation Group remains intact, with most of us now enjoying our golden years.

SEVEN
Loss of a Friend

F ischer Black's early passing came as no surprise to his friends. We knew he was gravely ill with cancer. Nevertheless, when I came across his obituary in *The Times* I experienced a real pang of sadness.

We spent a lot of time together in Chicago, Cambridge and New York, usually over a meal. Mostly we talked about real-world applications of finance theory. When it came to finance theory, I was not in his league, of course. He was one of the great theorists of his time and I was a ham-and-egger by comparison. We clicked nevertheless.

Perhaps our affinity stemmed from challenges we had separately faced in pursuit of academic degrees. I described how beer-drinking with my fraternity brothers and long hours at *Harry's* poolroom competed with book-learning for my attention while working on my A.A. degree. It turns out Fischer had been expelled from the Ph.D. program at Harvard University because he could not decide on his dissertation topic. He vacillated among physics and mathematics and computer science and artificial intelligence, much to the consternation of the authorities. He finally settled on AI and

Harvard accepted a dissertation from him. Soon after that he abandoned AI to teach himself financial economics. Within a few years he was invited to be a tenured professor of finance at the University of Chicago, having taken nary a course in the field.

Like me, in other words, Fischer proved to be something of a late bloomer—a couple of peas in a pod, we were.

Although Fischer struck many people as a bookish sort, he was keenly interested in practice. He eschewed the image of the academic, preferring his time on Wall Street to his years in the academy. I suspect the time he spent at Harvard, Chicago and MIT felt like incarceration compared to the Goldman Sachs years, when he thrived.

It has always struck me as ironic that arguably his greatest claim to fame was his role in devising the Nobel-prize-winning Black-Scholes equation for the pricing of options. Fischer's preferred means of expression was *language*, not the formulas that characterize academic finance. He wrote in tight, crystal clear sentences with almost no rewriting or editing.

He taught a course at Chicago and then at MIT known as Problems in Finance (and informally as "50 questions"). Some scholars sat through the course more than once. I asked one who had, why people did this. "Did the questions change?" I asked. "No, the questions were the same. It was the answers that changed." In this vein Fischer epitomized Ralph Waldo Emerson's essay *Self-Reliance*, in which Emerson wrote, "A foolish consistency is the hobgoblin of little minds...."

I was very fortunate to be able to spend so much time with him. More than anything I am grateful to Fischer for his inspiration. He inspired me to think free of boundaries, to let logic simply take me wherever *it* wanted to go. I also learned not to become unsettled upon arriving at seemingly odd conclusions. These were gifts I treasured.

In the end, Harvard laid claim to its once-troubled son. Fischer's service was held at Memorial Church in Harvard Yard. It was more sparsely attended than I had anticipated. Jack Treynor, who introduced Fischer to finance when they worked together at Arthur D. Little, the consultancy, delivered the eulogy with tears streaming down his face. I doubt there was a dry eye in the chapel. I did not attend the gathering held after the service. I would have been ill at ease there with people I didn't know or barely knew. My business with Fischer Black had been strictly a private affair.

EIGHT

The EnnisKnupp Years: 1981-2010

We filed articles of incorporation with the Illinois Secretary of State for the formation of Chicago Research Associates in December of 1980. While this was pending we located office space; we would be subleasing from the Pope Ballard law firm in the Arthur Andersen & Company building at 69 West Washington, across the street from Chicago's iconic Picasso sculpture in Daley Plaza. We heard from the Secretary of State when they rejected our articles. It turned out that the Chicago Research Associates name, which would have been a *really* dumb one for our firm, was taken.

We had about a week to resubmit the filing with the Secretary of State. You see, we needed a corporate board resolution pronto to secure the lease for office space we had lined up or we would lose it (and there could be no corporate board resolution without a corporation). This meant that in our next filing we had to be *sure* no one else was using the name we submitted so that the filing would go through without a hitch. To this end we used our names in the firm name. We originally sought to avoid this for fear that people would mispronounce it. In hindsight, and recognizing that we were forming what would emerge as a national professional services firm, using our names was clearly the right thing to do.

WHAT'S IN A NAME?

Ennis, Knupp and Gold, Incorporated, came to life on January 8, 1981, when I was 36 years old. Dorothy Gifford and the founders opened the doors on February 1.

On the subject of what the firm would be called over the years: When Ron Gold left the firm after four or five years to pursue his interest in real estate, we renamed it Ennis, Knupp & Associates and would subsequently use the EnnisKnupp logotype. Employees would refer to it as "EK" or "EKA." Outside the firm, and in particular within the investment management community, where dealing with the firm was all business, the firm was simply known as "Ennis," something I never quite got used to.

WHAT WE DID

The cornerstone of our work for clients was establishing *investment policy*. This boils down to identifying a target allocation to equity and fixed-income assets. The idea is to select that allocation that is compatible with the investor's risk tolerance. This work was widely considered the firm's strong suit.

You might think pretty much everyone would be clear on the starting point for this work, namely, knowing who *bears* the investment risk for a particular portfolio. You would be wrong. I discovered a remarkable and enduring degree of confusion on the subject, including on the part of fiduciaries charged with investing the assets. Public pension funds are a prime example.

A public employee retirement system (PERS) is commonly thought to bear the risk of the investment portfolio its trustees oversee. The actual bearer of investment risk is the taxpayer who stands behind the state which in turn stands behind the PERS. The PERS is merely an administrative instrumentality of the state. If the pension fund performs poorly, it is the taxpayer that feels the pain sooner or later.

There are other examples of this form of confusion, which are discussed more fully in Appendix 1 under the heading, "Who's on First?" The point is, if you are not even clear on who bears investment risk, how are you to know how much to take?

For a fuller discussion of my thinking on institutional investment policy, see Appendix 1.

The result of this first phase of work is a succinct, clear statement of investment policy.

The next level of our work consisted of devising an *investment management structure* to execute the policy. This means deciding on the number and types of investment managers to be employed to carry out overall investment policy. You can think of this as putting the right boxes on an organization chart before filling in the names. Most institutional investors employ far too many investment managers and do so to their detriment. We were effective in discouraging this practice among our clients.

A big part of our work was *manager selection*. In latter years, we had more than three dozen professionals engaged in the research of investment managers of every type.

Another important part of our work was *monitoring* the clients' investments and reporting to the client on their performance.

For clients without investment staff we acted as staff. For example, a complex asset restructuring requires knowledgeable, hands-on management of the process. Our people would step in to plan and coordinate this activity among all the parties involved.

We also routinely attended client committee and board meetings, often in a leadership role.

ETHICAL FOUNDATION = BUSINESS STRATEGY

We adopted an expression of ethical intention that I had heard attributed to McKinsey & Company, namely, *Put clients' interests first, the firm's second and personal interests third.* Upon delivering this catechism to new employees, sometimes I would lean forward, look the person in the eye and solemnly say, "Never, *ever* bullshit the client." Newcomers got it right away when it was put to them that way: *Never bullshit the client.*

This was sound business strategy as well as an ethical orientation. If the firm conducted itself as we imagined, clients would be more inclined to trust us. As we earned their trust, they would rely on us more heavily. This meant giving us more work and being willing to *pay* for it. *Forbes* did a piece on the firm on the occasion of its retention by the U.S. Department of the Treasury in connection with its Troubled Asset Relief Program (TARP). The *Forbes* article illustrated how the strategy of putting clients first worked for us as well as clients. In it, Richard Morais wrote:

> ...In 2005, it emerged that the Ohio Bureau of Workers Compensation's $14.3 billion State Insurance Fund (SIF) was awash in politically-tainted corruption, a scandal that ultimately sent people to jail. Besides losing $215 million in an unauthorized offshore hedge fund, SIF had handed $50 million to a politically connected dealer who bought everything from coins to Beanie Babies.

The Republican governor asked Thomas J. Hayes, an official skilled at turning around troubled state bodies, to clean up the mess. In June 2005, Hayes three-member board asked Ennis Knupp to find out whether SIF actually had $14.3 billion in assets, and, if so, what they should do. Ennis Knupp had 90 days to figure it out.

"More than anything else, you get the impression they are on your side," says Hayes. "They are not trying to cream fees. They have more than enough clients."

…[Among other things] Ennis Knupp was…tasked with reviewing and recommending the retention or firing of SIF's asset managers. Each review was costing Ohio tens of thousands of dollars, and it was dripping out, every few days, that yet another asset manager had been canned. The political fallout was brutal.

That's when Ennis Knupp recommended to Hayes that Ohio instead dismiss all asset managers without prejudice and park its assets in index funds until some future date, when an orderly decision on managers could be made. Ennis Knupp's elegant solution provided a face-saving exit for asset managers; it abruptly stopped the drip of bad news and lessened the political turmoil, and it cut considerably Ennis Knupp's own fees, charged to Ohio on an hourly basis.

"Unquestionable integrity and professionalism," says the retired Hayes. "If I had a personal portfolio of $1.0 billion, I would hire…[Ennis Knupp]." Multiplied by

700, that's precisely what the U.S. Treasury has opted to do.

EnnisKnupp accepted no fees from investment managers or any other source that might compromise its independence.

In the latter years of the firm virtually all new business came by word of mouth. We discovered that a side benefit of developing a good reputation was that it kept marketing costs down.

A NURTURING YET CHALLENGING CULTURE

The early years of the firm were difficult. There was no other firm to copy. We did not hire from competitors. We felt strongly about training people ourselves.

We often hired people right out of college. We encouraged them to enroll in the CFA program and we paid for it. After they completed that, we encouraged them to get an MBA at one of the local universities, and we subsidized that heavily. We even had business etiquette training, where folks learned how to introduce Ms. Jones to Mr. Cohen and which fork to use when dining with clients. (This proved to be surprisingly popular.) All the while, employees were coming up the ranks within the firm, being trained in our way of doing things.

It took about seven years to turn out a fully prepared, client-facing consultant. Meanwhile, competitors were trying to pick off our people because they were known to be well-trained. They did not get many. Employees making it through the first few years loved the firm.

The junior professionals worked long hours during our quarterly performance-reporting periods, crunching data and writing reports. A dozen or more at a time stood cheek by jowl in our production room when summoned over the intercom to inspect freshly-bound client reports, page by page, for the tiniest flaw. These sessions were known as QCing, and camaraderie abounded there. The whole firm had lunch together regularly. There were no stars. Teamwork became everyone's second nature. Many, many enduring friendships were formed among EnnisKnuppers.

For many years the firm operated with what I referred to as our no-policy vacation policy. In the beginning Jim and I had better things to do than keep track of employees' time off. So, we decreed the following vacation policy: "Go when you need to, come back when you're ready." This was a hit with everyone; alas, HR and legal professionals came along in later years and insisted on a more business-like approach.

We instituted a coaching, or what some would call mentoring, program. We provided the senior investment professionals guidelines to help them develop the juniors. Year-end reviews included a coaching assessment in which juniors would rate seniors on topics such as *Takes time out to teach* and *Shows a genuine interest in my personal development*. Some of our weakest coaches at the outset became our strongest later on.

After one of our not-so-profitable early years, Jim Knupp and I reflected on the cost of our commitment to developing our own staff, essentially asking ourselves if it was worth it. One of us said something to the effect of, *It seems our main business is developing human talent and we earn consulting fees on the side.*

There is no question now that the investment in our human capital was well worth it. My mind fairly boggles as I reflect on the sheer volume of high-quality work delivered and the steadfast devotion

TEACH!

As investment professionals from around the world attending a week-long educational seminar, you realize the value of ongoing education. I encourage you to be lifelong *teachers* as well as learners.

How do you do this? The next time you sit down with a more junior colleague to review a work assignment or research project, take time out to teach. A good place to start is by explaining why the work is important. All too often we simply ignore this, and yet we all want to be engaged in work that is important.

You can describe how the work relates to theory or practice more broadly. You can identify articles or experts that not only could help them understand the topic at hand but master it. In short, take a genuine interest in their personal development. Expand their thinking whenever practical. And gently challenge them.

What is the payoff? When you do these things, you educate your younger colleagues. You help them grow. And you help them find meaning in their work. Most important, when you do these things, you *inspire*.

So, dedicate yourself to being a teacher—an everyday teacher. It may not sound glamorous. But if you are successful at it, you will change lives, including your own.

Remarks of the author at the July 2013 Financial Analysts Seminar in Chicago upon presentation to him of the CFA Institute's C. Stewart Sheppard Award for outstanding contributions in fostering the education of professional investors.

to clients. Nothing better represents what EnnisKnupp was all about than the sweat of the people who so scrupulously built it.

Succeeding at EnnisKnupp was not easy. You had to be smart, hardworking, capable of growth and a team player. Plus, you had to overcome your fear of failure. Apropos of this, I am reminded of the occasion on which I took a junior colleague to visit a client to present work he had done. This was his first client presentation—a big deal in the firm. As we sat with the committee waiting for the cue to begin, I couldn't help but notice how nervous he was. I leaned over and whispered,

> "I know how you feel, Todd. I've been there many times.
> I have a few words that might help. Would you like to
> hear them?"
>
> "Oh, yes."
>
> "Don't. Fuck. Up."

He erupted in laughter. The tension vanished. He rocked the presentation.

"DFU" became something of a watchword among the junior professionals, a kind of benediction they bestowed on one another before the big first client presentation—like *Break a leg* in the theater.

OWNERSHIP

Jim and I always felt EnnisKnupp should be employee-owned. Allowing others to become owners and share in the profits was good for the retention of our fine people. It also enabled the firm to preserve the culture of a top-notch professional services firm.

When employees reached the associate level we allowed them to purchase the firm's shares at book value. If they left the firm, it bought them back at book value. In the interim they received distributions that allowed them to recover their investment relatively soon.

In later years we formalized and gave structure to employee ownership. At that point Jim had retired and I held the lion's share of the stock. We planned to establish two classes of owners, principals and associates. All principals would have the same level of ownership. The principals' stakes would be ten times those of the associates. I would accept book value for my stake. This would prove to be a matter of some consequence down the road. There would be more than 40 owners when we sold the firm several years later.

When it came time to execute the legal document for the share redistribution I asked Steve Cummings and Doug Patejunas to stop by my office. Steve was the firm's CEO and Doug a board member. Both knew me well, of course. Among other things, they knew that I did not (refused to) read legal documents. On my desk between us sat, unsigned by me, the thick shareholder agreement that would give effect to the share redistribution.

I said, "You fellas realize I haven't read this thing, don't you?"

They both nodded.

"We have always contemplated the firm would be employee-owned, with transactions at book value, right?"

More nodding.

"And book value is all I get for my stock in this deal, right?"

Nodding.

Me, patting the document, "Does this thing say that if someday down the road you guys flip the company for a potful of money, I'll get my fair share?" (Heaven only knew what that might have meant; I certainly had no idea.)

Nods.

I stood and they stood. We shook hands. I sat back down and signed the document.

PRICING

In 1981 fund performance evaluation clients were used to paying $10,000 to $30,000 a year for such reporting services. Many still paid by directing commissions from their funds. These so-called soft dollars obviated a direct cash outlay. We sought to avoid this practice owing to the potential for conflicts. We positioned our basic retainer consulting service at $20,000 to $25,000, cash. Our service was far more comprehensive and of much greater value than a computerized performance report. But the whole proposition of having an *advisor* on retainer was novel. Moreover, accepting a *cash* fee at this level was a challenge at first for many of the funds we called on.

As we enhanced our service offerings over time, we faced the challenge of getting retainer fees up to $100,000 or more in order to be profitable. In other words, we were constantly selling the clients on the full depth and range of service we could provide. In later years, when the work of firms like ours was widely accepted, retainers in the mid-six-figures were not uncommon. It is a long way from $25,000 to mid-six-figures, and it took about 25 years to get there.

SALES

A professional service firm's culture should be reflected in all its activities, including the way it sells its services. Other firms went about the sales process in the conventional way. You submitted a proposal that described the firm's history, philosophy, approach, strengths, personnel and typically included a client list. Then your firm and one or two others would appear before a committee for about 45 minutes and try to close the deal. At this point, in my opinion, the others would often go astray. They would stand before the committee and *repeat* the same stuff that they had put in the proposal, perhaps with the aid of a slick PowerPoint presentation.

There are two weaknesses to this approach. First, you are wasting valuable exposure to the decision makers. Second, and most importantly, you are *selling* to people who have to decide whether or not to *trust* you. We all know what it feels like to be on the receiving end of a well-rehearsed sales pitch. We are on our guard. We are not open. We are not...trusting.

Whenever possible we approached a finals presentation like this: We would get information from the prospect to help us understand their investment program as well as possible in a short period of time. This might include the current statement of investment policy, a recent asset allocation table, a list of investment managers and a recent performance report. We would put a team together to review the material and come up with what would be our principal recommendations were this a new client. These recommendations might be to introduce or substantially increase index fund investments; introduce or increase international diversification; and / or eliminate an unintentional style bet arising from their allocations to various active managers. In the finals presentation itself we would skip the preliminaries about our firm. We would take five minutes to explain what we knew about their investment program from our research and not more than 10 minutes to lay out our "recommendations" in bare bones terms. That left *them* half an hour to question the logic underlying our recommendations and for us to have a conversation. The beauty of this is that we were talking about them, not us; and we were talking about investment concepts, not how great *we* were. This approach gave them an opportunity to "road test" us.

One memorable pitch was to the board of trustees of the Colorado state pension fund. This would be an important piece of new business for the firm. The meeting took place in a large conference room overlooking the Mile-High City. The executive director and chief investment officer escorted our team in and sat us at the foot of the table—all very formal. The trustees were government employees and elected officials. All sat stiff and expressionless, which came as no surprise. The board chairman asked us to begin our pitch.

We did not say, "Good morning." Nor did we tell them it was a privilege to appear before them. Nor did we tell them how much we enjoyed skiing in Colorado.

Without a word, we passed out a single sheet of paper with four or five topics on it. These were complex topics that might come up in an investment committee meeting or be studied at length by the staff. When everyone had the sheet of paper in front of them, I spoke. "Ladies and gentlemen, before you is a list of topical issues that investment trustees like you are faced with today. We would be happy to discuss any or all of them with you." And I stopped.

The trustees simply stared at me as if to say, *Are you kidding? Do you really expect to engage us in dialogue?* The staff was agape, horrified. They wanted to see EnnisKnupp get the business. And here we were blowing it by not putting on a proper dog-and-pony show.

We all waited. And waited. The room remained silent. At great length a gentleman at the other end of the table spoke up. Well, yes, he had an interest in one of the topics. I explained the topic briefly, in plain English, for the benefit of all the trustees. I discussed the pros and cons of it as a course of action in simple, clear terms. Someone asked if we recommended this or not. I answered frankly and directly. Then there was a question about another topic. And so it went. A lively conversation involving many of the trustees developed. Just before the chairman interrupted the discussion to point out that we were well over the 45-minute time limit, someone asked about a variant on a funding approach that I had never heard of; she wanted to know what we thought of it. I looked at her for a moment and replied that I had never heard of the practice; I would have to think about it before commenting. I did say, rather as an aside, that I was pretty sure that when I *had* studied it and had it figured out, I'd think it was a *bad* idea. Everyone in the room chuckled. I knew the business was ours before we stood up to leave the room.

Straight talk does not always get you what you want in sales. Our pitch to the investment committee of the New Jersey Investment Council made that clear. The committee chair, a hedge fund manager in his day job, asked if we thought hedge funds and other alternatives should be a principal thrust for the fund going forward. (New Jersey had made no alternative investments as of that date.) We said we thought that the fund's comparative advantage lay elsewhere, namely, in driving costs down. I saw the chairman wince ever so slightly and immediately knew our goose was cooked. (New

Jersey proceeded to establish a 12% hedge fund allocation, which proved a costly failure and is being wound down.)

You win and you lose in sales, with or without candor; so you might as well make it easy on yourself and talk straight.

The keys to selling professional services are (1) *be* the product and (2) earn trust. Let the competition try to convince the buyers that they are polished salespeople.

CLIENT RELATIONSHIPS AND THE WORK OF THE CONSULTANT

We envisioned delivering the highest quality work based on sound theory and empirical evidence. The work was to be delivered in a one-firm environment that put a premium on teamwork and ensuring that all clients got the same advice, circumstances warranting. So how did we do this?

EnnisKnupp operated from a single office even when there were more than 100 clients spread about North America. This was important to maintaining the firm's one-firm culture. It was also good for training, quality control and supporting senior consultants. The central Chicago location made this feasible.

If a professional services firm is going to put the clients first it cannot employ a cookie cutter approach in its work. There were no computer-generated products or reporting. All the work product was delivered in the form of high-quality written reports, free of jargon and boilerplate. Moreover, we delivered the reports ahead of meetings so clients could digest our analysis and advice prior to discussing it with us. Early in the history of investment consulting some in the field were accused of employing smoke and mirrors in the delivery of their work. We would not be accused of that.

Producing work product of this quality was challenging. For one thing it meant the entire consulting staff would have to write reasonably well. *Aargh!* New employees were furnished with three books. One was Strunk and White's *Elements of Style.* Another was William Zinsser's *On Writing Well.* The third was a collegiate dictionary. Everyone experienced having their work emasculated in peer review in the interest of making it intelligible to the reader. Writing and producing reports became the bane of many of our consultants. If anything drove a few good folks from the firm it was probably this.

The firm's senior consultants, called relationship managers, saw themselves not as experts but as *educators* and *helpers.* They realized that more than anything our work product and client meetings served to help clients develop a sound enough understanding of our ideas to act upon them. Once a course of action was decided upon, we helped the client implement and monitor it. Educators-and-helpers is what we were when we were at our best.

We were especially wary of recruiting people who fancied themselves as experts. We knew that to be effective in our rather humble line of work as educators and helpers there was no place for ego.

CLIENTS

Some of my client relationships predated the founding of EnnisKnupp and continued throughout the firm's 30-year history. I had the good fortune to work with a wide variety of clients types, including:

Corporate and Partnership. Long-term clients with whom I had initiated relationships back in the Becker days included Ernst & Young, Leo Burnett Co. and Maytag Corporation. These three companies were like family—we were a part of theirs and they were a part of ours.

Leo Burnett Co. was the famed creator of the Marlboro Man, the Maytag Repairman, Tony the Tiger, the Green Giant and a bunch of other beloved characters and "critters" of American advertising. Their corporate culture was much like our own, and all our folks enjoyed working for them.

Things were getting off track at a Burnett investment committee meeting one morning, and Jack Kraft, the CFO, was unhappy about it. Our day-to-day contact at Burnett, Jerry Avery, and I really could have done a better job of advancing a particular investment proposal toward a sound conclusion. The guys at Burnett were a hard-charging bunch of advertising men, and Jack did not want to lose control of the meeting. So he called a break.

He took Jerry and me into a smaller room down the hall and laid into us. He was red in the face and screaming. He barked at Jerry to get things back on track and to do it quick. Then he turned to me and yelled, "And *you!* Ennis. You keep your damn mouth *shut!*" (Which, being no dummy, I did.) Only when you are family can you be taken by a client to the woodshed like this.

I also advised Arthur Andersen, Blue Cross Blue Shield, Citicorp, the Chicago Mercantile Exchange, Eli Lilly and Company, FINRA, Keebler Company, IBM, Intel and United Technologies.

Foundations. I advised the MacArthur Foundation from its start-up, when the trustees were not even sure what all John MacArthur owned at the time of his death and had not a clue as to its value.

Other foundations I advised included the Lucie and André Chagnon Foundation of Montreal, the Knight Foundation, the Mary Black Foundation, the National Merit Scholarship Program and Rotary International.

Cities and States. I advised pension funds or legislatures of Alaska, Arizona, Colorado, Florida, Hawaii, Illinois, Maine and Ohio. (Others in the firm advised several other state funds.) I also advised funds of Baltimore County and the City of Chicago for many years.

Shortly after the firm was retained by the Policemen's Annuity and Benefit Fund of Chicago, I received a call from Marshall Korshak, the board president. Mr. Korshak was a legendary pol from the old Democratic Machine era, who City Hall payrollers still greeted as "Senator" from his days in the Illinois State Senate. He was a lion in winter but still showed up at his law office every day to putter.

"Ennis, get over here, I need to talk to you." Right away I walked across the Loop to his office. Seated across from him at his desk I said,

> "What can I do for you, Mr. Korshak?"
>
> "Do you know what your job is over at the coppers' fund, Ennis?"
>
> "Well, yes, advise on investment policy, help select investment managers...."
>
> He cut me off with a roll of the eyes. He then reached into a desk drawer and removed a tattered, yellowed edition of the *Chicago Sun Times.* The front page consisted entirely of the following: A screamer that read, "Feds Raid Police Fund," bordered by photographs of the members of the board of trustees. His photo was prominent, top-center.
>
> It turned out to have been a rather minor IRS inquiry that had taken place many years earlier. But in Chicago,

it was fair game for a splash on the front page of the city's tabloids.

Once I had taken this in Korshak said, "Ennis, your job is to make sure *this* never happens again." And that was it.

Unions. The UAW Retiree Medical Benefits Trust had 90 days to set up a $20 billion investment program from scratch. The Trust came into existence as a result of a court-approved settlement consolidating carryover retiree healthcare funds from the Big Three automakers. It happened abruptly.

Each of the three healthcare funds had their own complex, multi-manager investment programs that were being managed by the automakers. Eric Henry, freshly appointed executive director for the Trust, without so much as an office or a desk yet, called out of the blue to ask if this were even possible. I assured him it was *not* possible to consolidate three complex investment programs so quickly. Then I told him we would take the assignment.

We began the next day with 15 professionals on the engagement. We worked long hours and weekends. We wrapped up on December 31, 2009, the day before the Trust went live without a hitch.

I advised the Central Pension Fund of the International Union of Operating Engineers from the late 1970s until my retirement in 2010. CPF was another member of the family.

I also advised the Pennsylvania Education Association and one of the Graphic Arts International Union's national funds.

Jim Knupp and I loved our union fund clients. They were loyal as can be once they trusted you. I was introduced to a man at a conference at which I was a speaker. He was a workaday union trustee, which became apparent when we shook hands and I discovered his palm was heavily calloused. Our brief exchange went like this:

He said, "I've heard of you."

I said, "Oh, yeah, what have you heard?"

He said, "Oh, I heard, uh…. You know, they say, uh…." and finally he said, "I heard you ain't a crook."

It doesn't get any better than that in the eyes of working folks charged with safeguarding union finances.

Religious. For many years I advised the United States Conference of Catholic Bishops in connection with Church moneys in the U.S. After I had resolved a difficult issue with one of their investment managers in a very satisfactory way, one of the bishops thanked me and told me that I had handled the matter like "a Vatican diplomat." It doesn't get any better than that for the men in black.

I also advised the Princeton Theological Seminary and the Christian Theological Seminary.

Cultural. I advised the Chicago Symphony Orchestra, the Museum of Science and Industry, the National Humanities Center, the Shedd Aquarium and the Wadsworth Atheneum.

Other. Other clients I advised included Butler University, CFA Institute, The League of Voluntary Hospitals of New York, Mount Auburn Cemetery, the country's first, in Cambridge, the Public Policy Institute of California, Spelman College, Stanford University, the U.S. Department of Labor and the Ohio Workers Compensation Fund, where we cleaned up after the scandal mentioned earlier.

That was an interesting project, to be sure. The CFO of the Ohio Workers Comp fund had turned the insurance operation's $14 billion investment portfolio into his personal piggy bank and went to prison for it.

He accepted bribes to appoint investment managers.

He had set up an internal "trading desk" and required the fund's investment managers to call that desk to arrange to have orders executed. The "traders" would then relay the orders to brokers chummy with the CFO. I have no firsthand knowledge of what emoluments he might have received in return for this consideration.

He employed a well-known consultant to "report" on investment performance. In reality, the CFO simply passed on to the consultant rates of return for individual investment managers that the managers themselves had provided to him—no checking was done by anybody. As for the total fund's rate of return, the CFO simply made that up—at twice its actual value. I was as astonished by the consultant's laxness as much as I was by the CFO's brazenness.

What made this assignment interesting was the discovery process. There was no paper trail and the investment department's files were in shambles. In effect our team had to camp out at the client's offices in Columbus and *discover* all this man's extraordinary contrivances to dupe and defraud his employer. As we caught on, we put an end to them.

LOVE FEST

The firm's clients gathered annually in the fall for a conference at one of the grand hotels on Chicago's Gold Coast. We had world-class speakers, including Jack Bogle, Steven Levitt (*Freakonomics*), Burt Malkiel (*A Random Walk Down Wall Street*), Bill Sharpe and Richard Thaler. Notwithstanding all the big names, the conferences were exclusively for our clients, which gave them the feel of distinctly private events. Indeed, the EnnisKnupp annual client conference was a low-key and genuinely *friendly* affair. We were gratified to see that the clients appreciated us as much as we appreciated them.

IDEAS, IDEAS, IDEAS

Writing was a big part of my professional life. It was driven by my preoccupation with *ideas*. People and things were important to me, yes; but processing ideas is what made me tick. I began to write in the early 1970s while I was working at O'Brien Associates. When I developed an interest in an idea, I would start writing about it as a way of satisfying myself that I understood the issues. Others found some of my early work interesting and provided encouragement.

My first published work was the monograph *Spending Policy for Educational Endowments,* co-authored with Peter Williamson of Dartmouth and published by Commonfund. In the early 1970s college and university endowment funds were transitioning to so-called total-return spending rules as a way of determining annual spending. Previously, they had spent whatever their portfolios' dividend and interest income happened to be. Peter's and my work was to evaluate the economic efficiency of various spending rules in use at the time. The work was well-received.

A satisfying aspect of my work as a generalist investment consultant was the broad range of topics I could write about. These included:

- "South African Divestment: Social Responsibility or Fiduciary Folly?" *Financial Analysts Journal,* July/Aug 1986
- "Is a Statewide Pension Fund a Person or a Cookie Jar?" *FAJ,* Nov/Dec 1988
- "Foreign Bonds in Diversified Portfolios: A Limited Advantage" (with Paul Burik), *FAJ,* Mar/Apr 1990

- "Pension Fund Real Estate Investment Under a Simple Equilibrium Pricing Model" (with Paul Burik), *FAJ*, May/Jun 1991
- "The Structure of the Investment Management Industry," *FAJ*, Jul/Aug 1997
- "The Case for Whole Stock Portfolios," *Journal of Portfolio Management*, Spring 2001
- "The Small-Cap Alpha Myth" (with Michael Sebastian), *JPM*, Spring 2002)
- "A Critical Look at the Case for Hedge Funds" (with Michael Sebastian), *JPM, Summer 2003*
- "Private Equity in Asset Allocation" (with Michael Sebastian), *Journal of Private Equity*, Summer 2005
- "Parsimonious Asset Allocation," *FAJ*, May/Jun 2009
- "The Uncorrelated Return Myth," *FAJ*, Nov/Dec 2009

I needed help whenever there was a significant analytical dimension to my research and writing projects. I understood finance theory well enough, but I am an intuitive person not conversant with formulas or programming. Consequently, I was reliant on the talents of our experts in quantitative finance. Michael Sebastian and Sudhakar ("Doc") Attaluri made my work in this area possible. Thanks, Mike. Thanks, Doc.

ADVISORY THEMES

Advisory themes played a vital role in the work. We wanted all the clients to get the firm's best thinking. As a means to that end we set out the firm's position in various areas so that clients got the same advice, circumstances warranting. There were never more than half a dozen or so positions or themes, many of which derived from our research and writing. We tried to put them down on paper from time to time, but that proved superfluous. The positions were forged in our internal discussions and day-to-day work. We knew them like we knew our own names. Here is a brief description of some of the most enduring EnnisKnupp advisory themes.

Indexing. Our advice to new clients was to put one-half their portfolio in stock and bond index funds as a start. The evidence in support of this approach began to emerge in the mid-1960s and was cumulatively overwhelming. A corollary to the 50%-indexed position was to then increase or decrease the indexed percentage based on the collective success of active managers over time. Clients that did this saw the passive percentage of their assets rise fairly steadily, with some approaching 100%.

Avoid Closet Indexing. The term "closet indexing" originated to describe a portfolio manager's hugging the benchmark to guard against significant underperformance. It can be applied more broadly, as well, to investors that use too many active managers to their own economic detriment.

"Diversifying" among active managers is insidious and wasteful. The standard practice was to use several active stock portfolio managers with "complementary" styles. It was not uncommon to see 10 or more active strategies combined in this fashion. Here we did two things. First, we published an article in the *Journal of Portfolio Management* demonstrating empirically the failure of "style diversification" in fund-of-manager funds. These were pooled investment funds constructed by experts using numerous sub-managers with differing styles. The funds we looked at underperformed their benchmarks by an average of 1.3 percentage points a year, an amount approximately equal to their expenses. The result did not surprise us.

The other thing we did was to create software to quantify the effects of closet indexing in our clients' own portfolios. The *Implied Expectations* model, as it was known, illustrated for clients their expected gain, or "alpha," from active management given their collective active investment exposures and degree of diversification. This usually amounted to just a few basis points per year *before* fees. It was the inevitable result of having a collective style exposure similar to that of the market plus very broad security-level diversification. In other words, it is hard to perform very differently from the market when your "active" portfolio closely resembles the market.

The cure for closet indexing is fewer managers, more concentrated managers, more indexing or a combination of the three. This was our prescription.

Foreign Stocks. Roughly half of the common stock opportunity set lies outside the United States. It is too large a segment to ignore in achieving efficient diversification. Recognizing the importance of peer comparisons in performance evaluation, however, we were cautious not to overdo international diversification. Accordingly, we typically recommended that non-U.S. equities—in developed and emerging markets—constitute approximately 20% of total equities. This was more progressive than the typical allocation but not extreme.

Foreign Bonds. We advised against a policy allocation to non-dollar bonds. The currency risk of such bonds more than offsets the benefit of diversifying interest rate movements across country markets.

Active Managers. A manager research analyst can consider many things in evaluating whether or not a particular active manager is likely to beat the market. One criterion was paramount in EnnisKnupp's evaluation of active managers, namely, the nature of a manager's comparative advantage, or *edge*. Active money management is highly competitive. Markets are efficient enough and costs are such that a manager needs more than really smart people and the other attributes their marketers customarily trumpet. The manager needs something others do not have and cannot easily acquire—an edge.

We were skeptical of the conventional wisdom that smaller stocks tend to be ignored by analysts and were thus a fertile area for active management. We presented our research findings to the contrary in the *Journal of Portfolio Management* in an article titled "The Small-Cap Alpha Myth" that won a Bernstein Fabozzi Jacobs Levy Award.

Hedge Funds. One-and-twenty or two-and-twenty should have been enough to scare off investors experienced with active management of securities portfolios. That level of charge is a staggering burden. Our research, published in *JPM*, and earning an award there, provided other reasons to avoid hedge funds. For one, they are not market neutral; portfolios of multiple hedge funds exhibit significant exposure to various market factors. Another problem arises from the stale pricing of less liquid hedge fund assets, which gives the illusion of low volatility. Finally, the performance of diversified hedge fund strategies had been lackluster when costs, risks and liquidity were accounted for.

EnnisKnupp's use of advisory themes served the firm well. They provided a means of ensuring all the clients got our best thinking. They also helped to establish the firm's identity.

CHARACTER COUNTS

Character counts in consulting. It not only counts, it is *huge*. Clients count on a consultant to give them her firm's best thinking. And yet she invariably finds herself telling someone something they do not want to hear. That someone often has a say in whether the consultant will continue to be employed, which is to say, with candor comes some risk. But the only thing worse than smoke and mirrors in consulting is the consultant that blows in the wind. A great consultant learns to combine tact with candor, and she works to help the client to do the best it can with at least the tenor of the advice.

There are times when the difference between consultant and client goes beyond differences as to the merit of the advice. It did not bother me when a client declined to accept our advice. But it bothered me a great deal when it became apparent that one or more of the trustees was disposed to act in a manner contrary to their legal and moral duty to protect the interests of the beneficiaries. When circumstances require it, the consultant should speak out. If worse comes to worst she needs to be prepared to exit.

One such case involved an unsavory character who was the chairman of the finance committee of a union pension fund client. On a day that the fund's other powerful trustee was absent, the chairman sought to have an investment manager hired to manage an account for the fund. But he ignored the fund's policies for the hiring of managers. He arranged for what proved to be a crony of his to appear unscheduled and unvetted before the committee to make a pitch. As that man was leaving the room I said to my associate, *Gather up your things, Judy, we're leaving.* I then turned to the chairman and said, "What you are doing is wrong. We won't be a party to it. Good day, sir."

My associate and I stood and headed for the door on our way out of the building. As we departed the chairman shouted, "And good riddance, Ennis!" (We had tangled before.) As it turned out, the trustees did not hire the manager. Furthermore, when things cooled down, our relationship with the fund continued on, as healthy as ever.

In another case, things worked out differently. We made the trustees of a state pension fund client aware of serious irregularities in the management of investments on the part of a key staff member. This situation went unaddressed over the course of several months and multiple board meetings. The trustees were inclined to overlook the problem. We made clear that that was unacceptable to us and offered our resignation. At great length the board reluctantly accepted it. And that was that. These things happen in the course of providing professional services. You learn to take it on the chin.

"EXPERT"

I did a fair amount of expert witness work during the EnnisKnupp years. Mostly it dealt with whether or not an investment fiduciary had discharged his or her duties of prudence and loyalty to the beneficiaries of the trust they served. The bulk of the work was for the U.S. Department of Labor in connection with actions it brought as part of its enforcement of the fiduciary provisions of ERISA, the pension reform act.

Virtually all the funds we worked for were trusts that had a supervisory board. The members of those boards were fiduciaries to the beneficiaries of the trust. The body of fiduciary law in the U.S. dates back to the Prudent Man [sic] Rule established in Harvard College v. Amory in 1830. The judge there said things were always changing so there could be no fixed, enduring standard in judging a trustee's actions. Rather, he or she should be judged in light of how *prudent* trustees in like circumstances conducted themselves. In other words, to allege a trustee had acted imprudently you had to know how prudent trustees generally acted under similar circumstances. That was where I came in.

I sat with and counseled investment trustees for a living. I understood their intentions and aversions. I knew what made them tick in connection with the decisions they made. This knowledge was useful to plaintiff and defendant counsel in fiduciary litigation.

After handling a number of cases I concluded that this work was not a good use of my time. I discovered that judges would not rule in favor of plaintiffs except in the most flagrant situations, and sometimes not even then. In one case an employer contributed to his company's retirement fund two adjacent parcels of undeveloped land with no income, uncertain value and no immediate prospects. The employer did this in lieu of making a cash contribution to the fund, which was customary. These were the only two assets in his workers' trust fund. This constituted a blatant violation of the standard. Prudent trustees did not hold vacant land; they held liquid, income-generating stocks and bonds. And they extensively diversified their holdings. In this case the Department of Labor attorneys were arguing rightly that the action violated ERISA's explicit mandate to diversify employee benefit funds. Counsel for the defense pointed out that the employer *had* diversified by virtue of contributing *two* vacant lots. The judge, evidently not wanting to appear overly zealous on behalf of the exercise of prudence, ruled in favor of the defendant.

It was just as well I gave up on being an "expert." It created more time for research and writing.

INSIDE THE BELTWAY

One afternoon I received a call from a gentleman, Mr. Smith I will call him. He was with the Department of Labor In Washington,

D.C. He was calling on behalf of the Secretary. Mr. Smith informed me that the Secretary wanted to have me named to the ERISA Advisory Council. The Secretary had received my name from an organized labor executive in D.C. Mr. Smith had checked me out and they wanted to proceed with the appointment.

In those days the President of the United States actually made these appointments, and the White House would have to sign off on mine. I should expect a call from someone there, Smith said. Smith was calling to prep me for that call. The balance of our conversation went like this:

> "Mr. Ennis, we've checked you out pretty thoroughly. When the White House calls they will ask you a question. It is a question they are not *supposed* to ask you, but one which we know, from experience, that they *will* ask. I am calling to help you prepare for that question."
>
> "Okay. Fire away."
>
> "Who did you vote for in the last presidential election?"
>
> "John Kerry."
>
> "That's the wrong answer, Mr. Ennis."
>
> "What do you *mean* it's the wrong answer?"
>
> "I mean you will not get the appointment if you say you voted for the President's opponent."
>
> "Well, what am I *supposed* to say?"
>
> "You *could* say, 'I understand the Cherry Blossom Festival is in full swing. How is the Tidal Basin looking?' In other words, what you say doesn't really matter as long as it's *not* that you voted for the President's opponent. Here in the capital it's our way of signaling that,

while you may be from the "wrong" political party, at least you won't be a troublemaker."

"Are you shitting me?"

"No, Mr. Ennis, I am not shitting you."

I told Mr. Smith that I probably would not be a good fit for the ERISA Advisory Council. I thanked him for calling and asked that he express my appreciation to the Secretary for considering me. He said he understood and wished me a good day.

IMPROVED RELATIONS

A measure of the success of institutional investment consulting is that it spawned a related field of endeavor—consultant relations. I am referring to the growing cadre of investment professionals who manage the flow of communication between investment managers and consultants for the benefit of institutional investors. They make for a healthy dynamic between managers and consultants. It wasn't always so between these two breeds.

Recall the exchange I had with the CFA Chicago Society in 1975 when I wanted to join. Back then the investment profession was not at all sure it wanted to have anything to do with the lesser-pedigreed folks calling themselves consultants.

Things hadn't improved much by the time we founded Ennis, Knupp & Gold in 1981. One of the first calls I took was from a money management salesman I didn't know. He announced that he wanted his firm to be among our first clients.

"For what?" I asked.

"I am open to suggestion," he replied.

I politely informed him that the firm would not be accepting compensation from investment managers, which came as a bit of a surprise to the fellow. I never heard from him again.

The good news was that the value of consultants was beginning to be recognized. The not-such-good news was that we were still a long way from being recognized as *professionals*. And for good reason: most consultants in those days gladly took money from investment managers. The field of investment consulting had a lot of work ahead of it before attaining the status of profession. And as this began to happen, investment consulting gave rise to the field of consultant relations within the asset management industry.

I can't trace the precise origins of consultant relations as a specialty field. But I know where some of the seeds were germinated—at PIMCO, circa 1980.

By the late-70s Bill Gross had compiled a track record that had caught the attention of plan sponsors and consultants, putting him very much in demand. Bill began having a hard time wearing three hats—managing bonds, meeting with clients and making new-business presentations. PIMCO made a smart decision to keep him on the trading desk in Newport Beach and leave the relationship work to others.

So, who would represent the firm with the rapidly growing number of clients, prospects and consultants? PIMCO made another wise and innovative call here. They created a team of bona fide investment professionals to represent the firm to the outside world. These were fixed-income professionals, some with graduate degrees, some with CFAs, who had come up in the Pacific Mutual-PIMCO organization. When the first of these folks reached out to us my reaction was, *What's a person like this doing calling on us?*

Nonetheless, we soon became accustomed to dealing exclusively with dedicated investment professionals, by one name or another. Although originally known as "client relations executives" or something to that effect, these teams soon branched in two as it became evident that clients and consultants had distinct needs. But the die was cast; both constituencies had become accustomed to dealing with professionals.

The advent of consultant relations has been a very positive development. It has enhanced the reliability and integrity of the information received by the advisors to institutional investors. The manager-consultant interface is now more relational, less transactional, making it a much richer exchange of ideas and information. I am a big fan of the indispensable work these folks perform.

I do have a suggestion for all the up-and-comers in the consultant relations field. It is the same suggestion I made earlier to investment consultants in their new-business work: *Be* the product rather than try to *sell* the product. Earn the confidence and trust of your consulting counterparts. This is the key to building strong relationships.

How to do this? Three ways: Know. Embody. Help.

Get to know your firm and its strategies as thoroughly as you can. It is this knowledge that enables you to serve your counterparts effectively.

Study your employer's business—not only the people and the facts but the ethos of the organization. Seek to *embody* the firm—its values, its spirit—as best you can while remaining true to yourself.

Just as I described the best consultants as those who see themselves as helpers, I encourage you to see yourself in that way, too. And if you find yourself getting all salesey, just think about turning the bubble machine down a few notches.

▪   ▪   ▪

Two years ago I retained a firm to represent me in a real estate transaction. In my first interaction with the firm, the individual assigned to work with me made a salesey statement regarding a material fact. But it was over the line from salesey; it was patently false. She must have thought she was taking a minor liberty with the truth. I didn't; I fired the firm straightaway. I soon received a call from the head of the firm, wanting to know what went wrong. I told her. She said, "Oh, that's just the way we talk." *Just the way you talk??!!*

I realize I am an old retired guy who wouldn't know a "solution" from a "platform," and to whom much contemporary investment-speak sounds like so much blustery jargon. But we *all* have a pretty good ear for bullshit, don't we? So express yourself—in your own voice—earnestly and plainly.

THE YEARS ROLL BY

EnnisKnupp existed just shy of 30 years. We started in 1981 with four employees. The head count grew to 136 by 2010, when we sold the firm.

During this period the client roster grew to more than 150. A number of them had been with the firm for more than 20 years at the time of its sale. Assets under advisement had reached $2 trillion.

Jim Knupp retired. The firm accomplished a successful management succession when Stephen Cummings, a protege of mine, took the reins in 2000. Under Steve's leadership the firm built out robust specialty consulting areas for real estate, private equity and alternative investment strategies for clients needing that kind of specialized expertise. We were exploring overseas expansion.

Revenue during that period continued to grow at double digit rates. Profit margins were very satisfactory. Ownership expanded to more than 40 persons.

People at every level and in every capacity were justifiably proud of what we had accomplished. The future was bright as we approached the start of our fourth decade.

SOME TRAVAIL AND A SALE

Over the years we had been approached several times about transacting the firm. We always politely demurred. In 2009 we were approached a second time by Hewitt Associates, a large and well respected, publicly-traded human resources firm that had long admired EnnisKnupp. They had their own investment consulting practice but had been unable to get the traction they wanted and needed for a firm their size. By that time EnnisKnupp was probably the biggest practice by any measure. There were more than 40 EnnisKnupp employee-owners—about 20 principals with equal shares and a like number of associates with equal shares a tenth the size of the principals'.

I had no interest in entertaining another approach by Hewitt. I recognized, however, that I was nearing retirement and there was likely to be a lot of money involved and a lot of people affected. So I took the expression of interest to our board of directors. The board decided that it had a responsibility to consider the possibility of a sale. I concurred even though I lacked enthusiasm for the idea.

Steve Cummings was the firm's CEO then. Steve was and is a fine man. The board charged Steve with representing the firm in discussions with Hewitt. Steve had accepted a challenge in leading the firm while I was still active. It was the classic dilemma faced by the successor to the visionary founder. He had to run the operation while the old boy was still around. During the years he was in charge he did an excellent job under difficult circumstances. Our relationship became strained but remained workable. Negotiations for the sale of the firm strained the relationship further.

The truth of the matter was that I really didn't *want* the firm to cease to be employee owned. Nor did I like being a bystander while it was auctioned off. And yet, as chairman of the board of directors and accountable to shareholders, I felt an obligation to let the process play out.

The negotiations dragged on for the better part of a year, during which time I confess I had become a thorn in Steve's side. I was, for example, cynical about the possibility of there being any synergies arising from a merger. Whenever Steve attempted to describe one at a board meeting, I would snort, "The reason to sell the firm is for the money!" I was saying sarcastically, *Let's not kid ourselves about the reason for a sale.* Whether the other directors agreed with me or not, they all grew weary of hearing me carry on like this.

There were some serious snags. Steve and the lawyers worked through them. The offering price continued to rise through it all. The deal went through in the summer of 2010. In the process we minted more than 20 millionaires. Another 20 or so, mostly young professionals, received very significant payouts.

For his part, Steve did what was right for the employee-shareholders. He realized a price for the firm far in excess of what any of us thought possible. And, yes, I got my fair share.

There was an interesting twist to the transaction. During the course of our negotiations with Hewitt, unbeknownst to us, Hewitt had entered into merger discussions with Aon, the much larger global insurance enterprise. The two sets of negotiations came to fruition at the same time; we would become part of Hewitt (if we elected to go through with the deal) just as Hewitt was becoming part of Aon. Aon, as things would have it, had been an appreciative EnnisKnupp client. Its CEO, Gregory Case, knew our firm. He was delighted to learn that an EnnisKnupp "bonus" would come with his purchase of Hewitt. EnnisKnupp indeed turned out to be a bonus. In a few years Aon spun-off a big chunk of Hewitt but retained the investment consulting business. That is how EnnisKnupp came to be known first as Hewit-EnnisKnupp and then as Aon Investment Consulting.

The sale of the firm clarified my retirement plans. I was 65. I was satisfied with my career. And I was tired of getting on airplanes. So, I retired on the day we closed the deal. Soon after that, with sons John, Colin and Ryan grown and on their own, Sally and I departed Evanston to live year round at our home on the beach of Sanibel Island.

■ ■ ■

It took a long time for me to come to terms with wrapping up, in one fell swoop, both my career and my association with the firm that had been an extension of me for 30 years. It was a *lot* to process.

On the one hand, I was ready to retire. I had long thought I would work indefinitely for the love of it. But the work was ceasing to gratify. I had begun to resent clients having me meet with them, regardless of what they were paying. I would rather have been working in my garden, reading a book, or pushing pool balls around in my basement. It was clear I was ready for a life of quiet with, perhaps, some low-key adventure.

Nevertheless, I was angry about the sale of the firm, and I stayed that way for a long time. While it was a financial windfall for a lot of people, including me, the great majority of employees felt that they were losing the job of a lifetime. Everyone knew that I could have put a stop to the sale process any time I wanted by virtue of my moral authority. The principal-level shareholders were ambivalent about the sale, even though their financial futures would be assured by it. They loved the culture and many benefits of a smaller firm they had helped create. The prospect of being employees of a much larger firm of actuaries and benefit plan administrators held little appeal. Everyone else was downright sick about it. A few people would lose their jobs owing to the inevitable redundancies in a merger. I felt terrible for them.

Right up to the end I was torn between keeping the firm independent and going along with the sale. In the end the financial steward in me said, *Let the deal play out and allow the shareholders to vote on it.* I did and they did. And that was that.

As the years passed, my unhappy feelings gradually dissipated. As the old saying goes, time heals all wounds. I have ill feelings toward no one. Everyone behaved honorably and earnestly. You can't ask for any more than that.

NINE

Occam Asset Management

What if I had not retired in 2010? What if I were 10 years younger when we sold the firm, and I had a bunch more airplane rides left in me? I had had enough of conventional consulting. I had no desire to be a part of a giant firm. I had written enough. So I would have to do something different.

I would have started a firm to manage institutional funds. Occam Asset Management would manage portfolios with the greatest economic efficiency possible. (The name is homage to William of Ockham, for whom Occam's razor of logic is named.) Occam would essentially be an outsourced chief investment officer, or OCIO in today's parlance.

The state of the art of institutional investment-policy-making had become muddled with myth and pseudo-sophistication by the time 2010 had rolled around. (This situation only worsened in the ensuing years.) Earlier I discussed the ills of "diversifying" with several active stock portfolio managers, which results in closet-in-dexing and steady leakage of wealth. Occam would do away with this problem by dispensing with active management altogether.

The firm's marketing tag line would be: *You want active management? Hedge funds? Private equity? Go someplace else.*

A second feature of Occam's approach would be to dispense with the black art of portfolio "optimization" and other forms of asset-allocation modeling. Sheer logic based on available facts would be the basis for determining an appropriate asset allocation for each client.

Occam would generally manage the client's entire portfolio. As the firm's principal I would develop a thorough understanding of each client's circumstances. I would do this by gathering information and employing a handful of considerations I have developed to think through an investor's situation to arrive at a sound investment policy. I would then decide on the asset allocation for each client—using a single blank sheet of paper, a No. 2 pencil with an eraser and maybe my slide rule. (Appendix 1 reveals some of my secrets.)

Occam Asset Management would be heralded widely as...*The firm where even the clients understand their investment policy.*

As for implementation, Occam's quiver would contain but three arrows:

- A short-term, passive government securities fund,
- An aggregate-type domestic bond index fund, and
- A passive, global, all-cap equity portfolio.

Occam would subcontract asset management. We would seek plain vanilla passive management in commingled or separate accounts—whatever was cheapest. We would have one or more sub-advisors with massive assets under management in order to deliver these mundane exposures at the lowest possible cost.

Clients would pay Occam an all-inclusive fee in basis points as a percentage of asset value. (A basis point is 1/100 of one percent.) Total management fees would be 5-10 basis points. Transaction costs would be next to zero. The all-in cost of operation would be about a tenth of the cost commonly incurred by institutional investors.

Owing to extremely low cost and broad diversification, client portfolios would invariably perform favorably in peer comparisons over the longer term.

Clients would have no investment staff. Portfolio rebalancing would be accomplished administratively through funds flowing in or out of the portfolio. Once a year Occam would review client circumstances and revisit asset allocation. Boards would meet once a year to review the program. Client organizations would get on with whatever it is they do best. Occam would not send clients so much as a box of chocolates during the holidays.

Yes, that is *exactly* what I would have done.

TEN

Financial Analysts Journal

inancial Analysts Journal was established in 1945. Benjamin Graham helped launch it, contributing an article to the inaugural issue. I discovered *FAJ* when I began working full-time at Transamerica in 1970. *FAJ* is a refereed journal published by the CFA Institute primarily for its more than 150,000 practitioner-members. Owing to the quality of its articles, and with thanks to its remarkable long-time editor, Jack Treynor, it also developed a following among scholars. It was the rare crossover journal between profession and academy. It was cutting-edge intellectually, yet not dense with Greek. *FAJ* played a crucial role in helping me update and advance the education I got in school. I began reading every issue cover to cover in the 1970s.

Over time I came to know many of the journal's contributors and other devotees. We formed a community of sorts. I referred to the most ardent among us as the *godparents* of *FAJ*. Whenever any of Jack's successor editors slipped up in any way, like publishing a dud of an article, he could expect to hear from one or more of us.

I tangled with two of Jack's successor editors. I felt one had done a great job for several years but then lost his way editorially, and I let him know it. I felt the other was talking his own book, in investment parlance, and I admonished him to knock it off.

The first paper of mine to be accepted for publication dealt with the subject of South African divestment, a controversial topic at the time. Counter to my liberal bent, I was against the practice, believing it violated trustees' fiduciary obligation to manage assets for the exclusive benefit of beneficiaries. The article was well-received and I was invited to present it to the Boston Society of Security Analysts at Faneuil Hall.

One of the proudest moments of my career was when colleague Paul Burik and I received the Graham and Dodd Award for the best article published by *FAJ* in 1991. The subject of the article was real estate investing in the asset-allocation context. The Graham and Dodd Award is the holy grail of publishing in the investments field.

Later on I was invited to join the journal's Editorial Advisory Board. This is a panel of industry and academic experts that serve as referees in the journal's editorial review process.

I was named Editor of *FAJ* in 2006. Upon the announcement of my appointment as Editor, I received a one-line email from one of the other godparents: *Congratulations. Don't fuck it up.*

When I took over at *FAJ* I met Rodney Sullivan, the journal's Associate Editor and a full-time employee of the CFA Institute in Charlottesville. Rodney really ran the operation. He managed the staff and reviewed all the manuscript submissions we received. He then made a recommendation to the Editor as to whether he thought the piece had potential. It was my good fortune to partner with Rodney at *FAJ*. He had apprehended the soul of the journal and knew all the godparents. He knew the literature and had excellent editorial judgment. He worked as hard as anyone I knew, reviewing manuscripts and managing the contributors and referees.

At that time *FAJ* received approximately 300 unsolicited manuscripts a year. We needed to find about 30 gems to fill out the six issues a year that we published. Alas, we didn't receive 30 gems in the course of a year. Of the manuscripts submitted we typically identified not more than 20 to 25 a year that we believed warranted publication. To get the rest Rodney and I would have to chase papers, something that would take up a lot of our time. We both stayed in touch with professors in the academy who were doing interesting work and would write for our audience. We attended gatherings like of those of the Q Group, where top-notch papers were presented, often for the first time. As a result of this effort, we were able to fill out the pages of our journal. Gratifyingly, the papers we chased were often among the finest.

Editing *FAJ* proved to be an avenue of continuing education for me. As editor it was my job to read a large number of papers that otherwise I never would have seen—and some I would have made a point to avoid. In the latter category were papers advancing the field of behavioral finance (BF).

I had been skeptical of the claims of BF. I was pretty much a mainstream efficient markets guy. Sure, starting in the 1980s I took note of papers challenging EMT that identified return *anomalies* inconsistent with rational stock-pricing. As a practitioner consultant I had also become keenly aware of the surge of investment products claiming to add value by exploiting anomalies. My impression was that, in general, managers of these products were no better at beating the market than other managers. So I had not paid the field much attention. (Later it occurred to me that the market does not have to be perfectly efficient for investment strategies to underperform; even an informed strategy can be sunk by its transaction costs and management fees. Thus, active-manager performance was an inadequate means of gauging market efficiency.)

By virtue of editing *FAJ* I was obliged to read a number of BF papers. I was particularly struck by the role *affect*—purely subjective liking or disliking in the field of psychology—might play in the role of asset-pricing. Eventually I concluded that affect provided an explanation of the performance differences between *growth* and *value* that was as or more plausible than any other I was aware of. "Spurned" company stocks outperformed the "favored" ones after adjusting for beta, small-minus-big, value-minus-growth and momentum.*

Reading papers on the role of affect in asset-pricing took me back in time to my days as a young money manager during the great growth-stock era of the late-1960s and early-1970s. Earlier I described growth-investing as the *ethos* of the times (ethos being defined as "the characteristic spirit of an era"). Seemingly without a second thought the mass of investors were paying 60-70 times earnings for: a chain of hamburger restaurants (McDonald's); a company that sold cosmetics door to door (Avon); and a mortgage insurer (MGIC). There was *no way* rational earnings-discounting could arrive at these valuations. I was unable to conceive of a better explanation than affect. It made sense and it *felt* right.

In the course of my work editing *FAJ* I concluded that there really *was* something to behavioral finance. I even managed to make this discovery before they started handing out Nobel prizes to people working in the field. Better late than never.

---

* See Meir Statman, Kenneth L. Fisher, and Deniz Anginer, "Affect in a Behavioral Asset-Pricing Model," *Financial Analysts Journal*, March/April 2008, Vol. 64, No. 2:20-29.

I liked writing the Editor's Corner. This is a space in each issue where the Editor writes whatever he wants in essay form. There I could speak to the investment profession at large in my own voice. And there I continued to expound on themes of economic efficiency and merit. For example,

> In "Big Bond Bust" you can hear me rail at bond managers for loading up client portfolios with nasty stuff in order to game the standard investment-grade performance benchmark. *Scoundrels!*

> In "The Uncorrelated Return Myth" I explain why the notion of garnering "uncorrelated" returns is hokum.

> In "Parsimonious Asset Allocation" I preach my simplified approach to asset allocation, by means of which investors can have low-cost, efficient portfolios using just a few investment "buckets."

A dozen of these editorials appear in Appendix 2.

After four years I realized I had nothing left to say and moved on from my beloved *Financial Analysts Journal*. I encouraged my successor to not, well, to not mess it up.

ELEVEN

The Sanibel Years

Jim Knupp and I had a conversation in 1999 in which he said,

"I know a place I think you and Sally would like to visit."

"Yeah, where is it?" I asked.

"Florida."

"We don't like Florida."

"This is different."

So, Sally and I booked a two-week stay at an oceanfront rental on Sanibel Island, Florida. By the end of the first week we had become the proud owners of a home on the beach there. There we would become snowbirds. And it was there, 11 years later, that Sally and I would head with our loot from the sale of EnnisKnupp.

Sanibel is a barrier island off the coast of Fort Myers, Florida, where the Caloosahatchee River empties into San Carlos Bay, forming a grand incubator of marine life. Most of the island is either national wildlife preserve or lands held in trust against development. There is a long tradition of ecological awareness on the part of island inhabitants. There are no traffic lights, fast food chains or buildings taller than a palm tree. People come from around the world to collect shells on the beaches. Sanibel has a sleepy, tropical, eco-friendly ethos all its own.

Early in retirement I wrestled with my identity. I had feelers about serving on boards of directors and consulting. I thought long and hard about continuing my research and publication work. Did I really want to continue as some form of Richard M. Ennis, man of affairs? I saw people in their 80s carrying on, or attempting to, as they had in the "prime" of their lives, and I cringed. In the end, I decided to let go of the past, and that just being "Rich" to long-time friends and Sanibel friends was good enough for me—a relief in fact. I allowed my wardrobe to go to pot in favor of T-shirts, shorts and sandals.

I spent plenty of time on the beach—walking it, playing in the surf and enjoying magnificent sunsets. With Sally I explored the J.N. "Ding" Darling National Wildlife Refuge, a well-known sanctuary for migratory bird populations. Sally and I would rent a boat at the marina for a run up to Cabbage Key for a cheeseburger at the rustic Old House. Some people say the mythical "Cheeseburger in Paradise" that Jimmy Buffet made famous in song originated there.

I opened my own pool room over John Nader's Great White Grill in a shabby little building that also housed the Goodwill. I modeled it after *Harry's* but on a smaller scale and minus the stench of stale tobacco smoke. There I enjoyed many, many delightful hours playing a game I love. I usually played alone, with just the click-click of the balls and my music for company. Sometimes I was joined by my great chum Bob ("Bunt") Buntrock. Every Thursday we—just the two of us —competed in the Pot Roast Invitational. Whoever lost had to buy lunch at Rich McCurry's Sanibel Cafe. Thursday's special: pot roast, of course.

Bunt enlisted me for his 8-Ball pool league team at American Legion Post 123, which is not much more than an island shack-bar. We, Bunt's Ball Busters, dominated the league for years. There I enjoyed great fellowship with Bunt, Gator, Jimbo, Butch, Doc, Big Kip and Little Kip, Johnny Earle, and Becky the bartender, to name a few. And, for the first time, I joined the American Legion.

Sally and I took up ballroom dancing. On a whim we wandered into a new dance studio on the island, Enchanted Ballroom. There David Flory, for whom we would develop great affection, began instructing us in ballroom. We discovered that not only could we dance, we enjoyed it—first taking up rumba, then foxtrot, waltz, swing and tango. We continue with weekly instruction, and we dance regularly at local supper clubs. I love dance. I love the music it has introduced me to; I love the expression of self; I love the flow. I made dance practice part of my exercise routine. I hope I die on a dance floor.

Sally and I discovered Key West and began to spend our Thanksgivings there. We toured Hemingway's house and drank at his favorite watering hole, Sloppy Joe's Bar. One evening we danced out in front of it in Duval Street to the appreciation of passersby. There I spotted a memorable sign on the side of a building: *Key West—a work-free drug place.* We dined high and low. "High" would have been Louie's Backyard. This is an old mansion with a sea wall on the Atlantic Ocean that featured fine cuisine, indoors or out (in the "backyard," overlooking the ocean). The "low," at least our favorite joint, was Charlie Mac's. A classic, open-to-the-breezes Key West bar, Charlie Mac's featured chickens wandering in off the street and pecking at what they could find on the cement floor among the barstools. We drank too much, laughed a lot and gorged on ribs, the house specialty. I especially enjoyed touring

Harry Truman's Winter White House. The interior had been scrupulously maintained. It really took me back in time.

Family reunions at Christmas were a highlight of the Sanibel years. Of course we were happy to have all our kids and grandkids with us. Cocktails on the beach at sunset were memorable. We had largely chaotic dinners in our home with plenty of drink, good food and music. The really great thing was seeing that everyone was genuinely having a good time and cared for one another. For parents it doesn't get any better.

Hurricane Irma in 2017 scared the daylights out of Sally and me. We evacuated to a bunker-like Marriott in Orlando as Irma roared toward Florida's Southwestern coast. We watched and listened as meteorologists on the TV assured us that if Sanibel Island were not blown away it would surely be washed away in a 12-foot storm surge. Miracle of miracles, Sanibel was spared. But the experience was enough to cause us to rethink our housing situation.

In 2018 Sally and I moved to Cypress Cove, which is located not far off-island from Sanibel. Our home is situated on a pristine lake. I was able to indulge my passion for interior design and art when we relocated here. Now I spend hours at a time in my sun-filled study, gazing out over the water, keeping tabs on the doings of Mother Nature. And it is here, well into my eighth decade, that occasionally I reflect on the past. I appreciate my good fortune, and I realize I am satisfied with life and career. In fact, I wouldn't change a thing if I could. And *that* is no B.S.

EPILOGUE

ntellectual curiosity animated my life's work. I sought answers to questions of economic fact and merit. I sought to communicate clearly what I came up with. I wanted to help clients. I wanted to move the investment profession in the right direction. I was always concerned with the big picture. Plus, I really *had* been inspired by Twain's encouragement to do the right thing—that it would gratify some people and astonish the rest.

I am certainly not the one to judge my efforts. Actually, most of the time it seemed to me as though I was hopelessly *lost* in the big picture.

I do know this: The most satisfying part of my work was interacting with other people—as mentor or in their service. It would please me to know that some of them were gratified by something I did. If anyone was astonished, well, that would be even better.

APPENDIX 1

A Heuristic Approach to Investment Policy

I have a recurring dream. In it I have the assignment of coming up with the investment policy for a great university's endowment fund. I am at a loss. So I set out on a cloudless evening with a lantern, not unlike Diogenes, wandering the university's campus. I am not in search of an honest man but Alma Mater, who I know will be recognizable by her unstylish and rumpled floor-length garment. I hope she will reveal to me the university's risk tolerance. And out of nowhere she appears, strolling serenely. She pauses. I raise my lantern and ask, "Alma Mater, can you tell me the risk tolerance?" Her gaze goes up to the heavens for a long moment. And then back to me. "Sigma of 10.9%," she murmurs, and continues on her way.

Oh, were it possible to glean an investor's risk tolerance so precisely and authentically!

■ ■ ■

When you read about portfolio theory in textbooks you encounter the concepts of *utility, indifference curves* and *risk tolerance*. I take all this as gospel even though, frankly, it is way over my head.

We do know that the appetite for risk varies among investors. The investment policy analyst seeks to match up as well as possible an investor's risk preference with that of the portfolio of choice. Erring significantly in either direction—too much or too little risk—would do the investor a disservice. So, as practitioners, we have to have a way of addressing the important, challenging issues that textbooks sum up so neatly.

What follows is a simplified description of my *method* for figuring out institutional investment policy in practical terms. It evolved over 40 years of practice as a consultant to institutional investors. My method melds finance theory and judgment. Experience moved me away from overreliance on formal (quantitative) finance models in my work with clients. They miss too much of messy reality. Mine is a heuristic approach—financial economics, yes, with rules of thumb, educated guesses and prudent judgment added, all orchestrated in a spirit of pragmatism.

THE ESSENCE OF INVESTMENT POLICY

In my work I reduce "investment policy" to the target allocation of assets between two types of investment. One is the class of publicly-traded, fixed-return securities. The other class, variable-return assets, are publicly-traded common stocks. This is the most elementary distinction to be made among investments. Either an asset provides a specified payment at a specified time or the return is uncertain in timing and size. Markets for stocks and bonds are huge and liquid. The essential return of either class can be captured in a portfolio of any size cheaply by means of an index fund.

So-called alternative assets—real estate, private equity, hedge funds —make up about 10% of the investment opportunity set. They are much less liquid than stocks and bonds. They do not constitute homogeneous groupings. By this I mean the systematic, or average, return component of the groups is unavailable to investors. Investors must expose themselves to idiosyncratic risks. This means one is challenged to treat them as an asset *class* in an economic analysis. In the full scope of the capital markets, alternatives are minor pieces—small in aggregate value, idiosyncratic in nature and expensive and labor-intensive to undertake.

One asset class after another has been introduced to institutional investors on the premise that it would dampen volatility and improve risk-adjusted return. These "risk reducers" have relied on the use of what I think of as an economically lifeless, or smoothed, return series to make their case. Real estate returns are based primarily on appraisals, not transactions. Private equity pricing relies heavily on acquisition or carrying values. Hedge fund returns often reflect the stale pricing of illiquid positions. One has to understand that if return volatility is to be used as a proxy for risk in decision-making, the returns must reflect genuine continuous-auction-market trading of the underlying asset. When smoothed returns are used in quantitative asset-allocation work they cause the attractiveness of the asset to be overstated, often by a wide margin.

For these reasons, in my work I reclassify assets other than stocks and bonds based on my perception of their equity-fixed character. Here is an example: Say an investor describes its policy as 55% common stocks, 8% commercial real estate, 2% private equity and 35% U.S. bonds. The first thing I do is restate these percentages. Upon completing a review of the particular real estate and private equity assets, I might characterize the former as half equity, half fixed. The private equity fraction might be re-characterized as equity at 150% of its nominal value, or 3% of portfolio value. When re-classifying and re-proportioning have been accomplished in the example, the result is 61% equity and 39% fixed.

The standard deviation of return associated with a particular stock-bond allocation is the common descriptor of risk. Say, for example the 61-39 policy has exhibited a standard deviation of return, or sigma, of 10.9% over the last 10 years. That is the statistical expression of policy risk.

"Equity" and "fixed" are solid categories of investment. When concentrating on the two principal categories, the process of asset allocation is a task in economics rather than an exercise in art or pseudoscience. An additional benefit of viewing investment policy this way is that it better allows one to make apples-to-apples comparisons among the policies of different investors.

THE UPWARD TREND IN RISK-TAKING

Greenwich Associates surveys institutional investors regularly. Table 1 indicates the allocation of assets they report for endowments as well as public and union pension funds. Greenwich employs 24 asset-class categories, which I have collapsed into two in order to clarify risk profiles and allow comparison among the different types of funds. ("Fixed" refers to fixed-income investments; everything else, predominantly common stocks, but including small amounts of private equity, real estate and hedge funds, is lumped under the "Equity" heading.) The composition of the global capital markets (per Aon Investment Consulting) is shown for comparison.

Table 1
ASSET ALLOCATION OF
VARIOUS TYPES OF INSTITUTIONAL INVESTOR

Asset Type	Endowments	Public	Union	Market
Equity	78%	69%	68%	51%
Fixed	22	31	32	49
Total	100%	100%	100%	100%

In the early 1980s both public and union funds had equity holdings of only about 25% of total assets. Their equity-type investments have increased by more than 40 percentage points since then. As recently as 1989 NACUBO reported the average equity percentage for endowments at 50%. The equity allocation of all three types has risen significantly in recent decades.

Table 1 also indicates that the three types of institutional investors have a decidedly more aggressive posture than the market as a whole, which is about 50-50 equity-fixed. In terms of conventional finance theory, this implies that the institutions are either (1) betting against the consensus view of asset-pricing in favor of equities, i.e., they are bullish, or (2) that they have a greater tolerance for risk than investors in the aggregate. A third and very real possibility is that the funds' aggressiveness is a sign of irrational exuberance and herding.

RISK BEARING: WHO'S ON FIRST?

The analyst needs to be clear on *who* bears the risk associated with the subject portfolio. One might think it would be obvious who bears the risk. In reality there is much confusion on the subject. I will try to clear up at least some of that confusion.

The bearer of risk of a public pension fund is not the retirement system that administers benefit payments and whose board of trustees may oversee portfolio management. Rather, it is the taxpayer who stands behind the state (or county or city) that stands behind the retirement system. The state makes pension promises (through legislation) and only the state has the legal authority to raise revenue to pay for the promises it has made. The retirement system is just an administrative instrumentality of the state. The pension fund is but one asset on the state's augmented balance sheet, just as pension liabilities are a single entry on the other side. (Public pension liabilities are grossly understated, by the way, but that is a different story.)

The taxpayer's liability in connection with the state's management of its finances is but one aspect of the taxpayer's own asset-liability calculus. The taxpayer's ability to reckon all this is questionable, and taxpayers generally do not have a say in the investment of public pension funds, anyway. But that is not an excuse for decision-makers to oversimplify the problem and mis-specify it by inserting the retirement system at the center of things as risk bearer. (Right, Ptolemy?) An implication of this is that conventional asset-liability modeling conducted at the retirement system level, while considered a so-called best-practice by many, is a pointless exercise.

The risk bearer of a single-employer defined-benefit pension plan is the corporate sponsor. The corporation is the maker of pension promises and is on the hook for them. Pension assets and liabilities appear on the corporation's augmented balance sheet. The corporation, not the pension plan, bears the risk. Fortunately, owing to developments in law (ERISA) and accounting standards regarding valuation of liabilities and their presentation on financial statements, the corporate pension fund investment problem is at least more tractable than is the case in the public sphere. (More on corporate pension fund investing later.)

Multi-employer (union) pension plan boards establish plan benefits based on negotiated contribution rates. Union plans have no recourse to employers for additional funding and are prohibited by law from holding surplus reserves. The plans are widely underfunded. In reality, union plans are DC plans contrived to appear to be DB plans. Plan participants bear the risk of union plans, and there is plenty of it to go around.

A college or university bears the risk of its endowment investments. But endowment risk is just one among the institution's bundle of financial risks. The proper risk framework is larger than the endowment fund, per se; it encompasses the institution in its entirety. Thus, investment policy must be resolved in the context of the institution, not just the endowment fund.

The board of an association I once advised considered the association to be the risk bearer of a large portfolio the board oversaw. My analysis revealed that the association *members*, not the association itself, bore the risk. In other words, the board had overlooked the true risk bearers. Prior to my involvement, the board's confusion on this matter had led it to adopt an investment policy that was overly aggressive and untenable for the association members. In 2008 the portfolio experienced severe losses. In the wake of this and with some chagrin, the board was forced to rethink things and revise the policy, which they retained me to advise them in doing.

Whether the investor is a public pension fund, a corporation, an endowed institution or an association, it is important to (1) be clear on who bears the investment risk and (2) understand how risk affects *them*. In summary, institutional risk bearers are:

- The taxpayer in the case of public pension funds
- The corporation and its shareholders in the case of single-employer pension plans in the private sector
- The plan participants in the case of private-sector multi-employer (union) pension plans
- The institution in the case of educational and cultural endowments
- Association members in the case of many associations

It may take some time and effort to figure this out in particular instances but doing so is vital. Going forward I use "investor" to refer to the bearer of risk.

RISK SENSITIVITY AND RELIANCE

In my work I take some liberty with economic theory in coming up with a heuristic for investor risk tolerance. Mine is *a measure of the importance in the investor's overall financial picture of the loss of a dollar of portfolio value.* I sometimes use the word *reliance* to refer to this measure of risk sensitivity. Reliance is an imperfect expression of textbook risk tolerance, but at least it gives the analyst something to go on.

I begin with the assumption that the investor is solvent, i.e., has a positive net worth. The specific risk-sensitivity metric I use is the size (dollar value) of the investment portfolio *relative* to the value of the investor's total liability. I use the term "liability" advisedly and in the economic sense of the term, not the accounting sense. For my purposes an investor's liability is the present value of all future cash outflows the investor anticipates during its existence. The *size* of an investor's portfolio is stated as a percentage ranging from close to zero to 100%. In other words, a portfolio of $100 million might be small *or* large in the investor's context; its size depends on the magnitude of the liability.

Let us look at a simple example of risk sensitivity, or reliance. Investor A has a portfolio that is a minuscule percentage of its liability. The value of Investor B's portfolio fully equals that of its liability. It follows that whatever happens to the value of A's portfolio will not have a significant impact on A's welfare. If B has no resources other than its investment portfolio, then a big loss in the investment portfolio could have a devastating impact on B's welfare. A's portfolio is *pin* money, so to speak, while B's is *rent* money.

Here is an illustration of differing degrees of reliance for two universities, a large public university ("Public") and a large private one ("Private"). Public has recently reported an annual budget of $6.5 billion and an endowment value of $2.54 billion. The corresponding figures for Private are $3.8 billion and $29.4 billion. Assume both universities contribute 4.5% of endowment to fund the budget annually, and both estimate that spending at that level will not erode the purchasing power of the endowment over time. Endowment spending would cover 1.76% of Public's budget and 34.8% of Private's budget. (See Table 2.) Private clearly has a lot more skin in the game than Public with respect to investing its endowment.

Table 2
Illustration of Investor Reliance (Risk Sensitivity)

	Annual Budget (Billions)	Endowment Fund Value (Billions)	Endowment Spending at 4.5% (Hundreds of Millions)	Endowment Spending as a Percentage of Budget
Private	$3.8	$29.4	$1,323	34.8%
Public	6.5	2.54	114	1.76

A third example might be a theological seminary that charges little or no tuition, funding the preponderant majority—say, 80%—of its budget from endowment spending. In institutional context, this is a *very* large endowment, regardless of its dollar amount.

Hypothetically speaking, an institution with a risk-sensitivity measure of just 2% may be well and prudently served over the long run with a portfolio invested entirely in stocks. Another investor, whose risk sensitivity measure is 100%, may be better served by limiting its common stock allocation to as little as 25%.

In passing, I note that the most conservative equity allocation I typically arrive at for long-term investors is about 25%. The benefit of stock-bond diversification is such that there tends not to be much if any advantage in reducing equities below that level for investors with a time horizon of five years or longer. By this I mean the imperfect correlation of stocks and bonds is such that an investor can operate with as much as approximately 25% in stocks while exhibiting a portfolio standard deviation no greater than that of bonds. This observation has led some analysts to say that, with equities, the first 25% is "free" in terms of its impact on risk, thanks to diversification.

AMERICA'S TROUBLED PENSION FUNDS

The risk-sensitivity logic described in the prior section assumes that an investor has a positive net worth. That is, the investor has assets—including those beyond the investment portfolio—that at least equal the investor's total liability, defined as the present value of anticipated cash outflows. This is the definition of solvency.

Public employee and multi-employer (union) plans do not conform to that model, and thus the model's logic simply does not apply to them. In a sense, public and union pension funds are both broke and broken; perennially large unfunded actuarial liabilities are endemic to them.

Overseers of these funds understand the dilemma. They talk more about their "need" for return than they do about their concern with risk. Public and union funds have seen their equity allocations rise steadily over the last 40 years, from roughly 25% in 1980 to nearly 70% today. Many trustees seem to believe they are somehow obliged to "do their part" to bring asset value more in line with plan liabilities—or at least keep the gap from widening. Increasing investment risk, though, has proven to be a strategy of hopefulness, desperation even. There is no way that more risk-taking is going to close the funding gap. As these portfolios' risk levels rise, public and union trustees may be probing the bounds of prudence in their management of the assets. And if there is cogent economic logic for their elevated risk-taking, it eludes me.

PEER PRACTICE

The emphasis I place on taking account of peer practice varies from case to case. I believe peer comparisons, in principle, have relevance for public pension funds. Here decision-makers (usually retirement system trustees) have great difficulty relating investment outcomes to the bearer of risk (the taxpayers). Agency issues and complexity are daunting. It is as if government-sponsored pension funds exist as free floating pools of long-term public capital, largely detached from economic context. There really is not much to guide decision-makers apart from trying to construct mean-variance-efficient portfolios as best they can. In their effort to do this it is not surprising that they would look around to see what others in their shoes have come up with.

American law encourages trustees to pay attention to the practices of peers. Justice Samuel Putnam established the precedent in handing down the Prudent Man [sic] Rule in Harvard v. Amory (1830). He wrote that a trustee should "…observe how men of prudence, discretion and intelligence manage their own affairs, not in regard to speculation, but in regard to the permanent disposition of their funds…."

Moreover, trustees often evaluate the performance of their fund in light of the results achieved by peers.

All of this is to say that peer practice has relevance in institutional investment, at least in some instances. For these reasons I consult surveys of investor practice to learn the average allocation among asset classes of similar types of investors. By no means will I hew to that information, but I will likely refer to it from time to time and it may influence my thinking.

With endowments and other simpler entities, I am inclined to place greater emphasis on the risk-sensitivity metric. There are two reasons for this. First, I can get at (determine) the risk sensitivity of these entities, i.e., characterizing investor context is more straightforward than is the case with, say, public pension funds. Second, risk sensitivity varies widely from institution to institution. In this domain I can envision the equity percentage ranging from as low as 25%, where risk sensitivity (reliance) is great, up to 100% equities where it is negligible.

In some cases peer practice is irrelevant. This is the case when the facts and implications of investor context come through loud and clear. One example is a corporate defined-benefit-plan sponsor interested in "de-risking" in anticipation of a plan termination. Here a bond portfolio custom-tailored to match the liability is indicated.

PASSIVE INVESTING

Once an equity-fixed (risk) policy is established, my advice to a new client would be to put *at least* one-half their portfolio in stock and bond index funds as a start. The evidence in support of passive institutional investing began to emerge in the mid-1960s and, over the course of more than half a century, has become cumulatively overwhelming. A corollary to the 50%-indexed position is to subsequently increase or decrease the indexed percentage based on the collective success of active managers over time. Clients of mine that have done this have seen the passively managed percentage of their assets rise fairly steadily, with some approaching 100%.

Really, people, it is high time that institutional fiduciaries responsible for conserving and growing other people's money push their passive investment percentages to 70, 80 or 90%.

CLOSET INDEXING

The term "closet indexing" originated to describe a portfolio manager hugging the benchmark to guard against significant underperformance. It can be applied more broadly, as well, to investors that use too many active managers to their own economic disadvantage.

"Diversifying" among active managers is insidious and wasteful. A standard practice among large funds is to use several active stock portfolio managers with "complementary" styles. It is not uncommon to see 10 or more active strategies combined in this fashion. In research published in the *Journal of Portfolio Management* I reported the performance of funds constructed by experts using numerous sub-managers with differing styles. The funds underperformed their benchmarks by an average of 1.3 percentage points a year, an amount approximately equal to their expenses.

The error of closet indexing is compounded in the public-fund sector. Taxpayers-as-risk-bearer are concerned with the *collective* outcome of pension fund investing in the jurisdiction. This gives rise to the fact that, as far as the taxpayer is concerned, there is a *single*, or unitary, state pension fund. This makes the case for indexing public pension investments even stronger. Consider the situation in California. The combined value of the two largest funds, CalPERS and CalSTRS, is well in excess of half a trillion dollars. They manage their assets independently of one another. Combined, they employ scores of active money managers for more than $100 billion of assets. In combination they constitute the grandest closet index fund on the planet. The waste in fees and trading costs is on the order of half-a-billion dollars a year. (Both funds, by the way, have underperformed a passive investment strategy over the 10 years ended June 30, 2018.)

The cure for closet indexing is fewer managers, more concentrated managers, greater indexing or a combination of the three.

SUMMING UP AND APPLYING THE METHOD

In thinking about institutional investment policy I make sure I am absolutely clear on who bears a portfolio's investment risk.

I start with the investor's *current* allocation of portfolio assets rather than a blank sheet of paper. Every investor's risk exposure evolves over time in a context that has relevance to the investor. This is not to suggest I will cleave to the past. But I want to know where the analyst that preceded me left off and to acknowledge the policy to which the investor has become accustomed.

My primary focus is on the equity-fixed allocation, which is the most important distinction to make. "Equity" and "fixed" are economically *solid* categories; all the others are comparatively soft in the context of investment policy analysis. In the example cited earlier, four asset classes were consolidated, leading to an effective equity-fixed allocation of 61% stocks, 39% bonds. That is the essence of the investor's risk profile.

Where possible I determine the investor's *risk sensitivity*, which I define as the value of the portfolio to the investor's *total* liability. In my experience, an extremely low level of risk sensitivity could prudently dictate an all-equity policy. An investor's appetite for risk may reasonably be expected to diminish as that measure rises.

In instances where I believe peer practice is relevant, I will take note of it. When the investor's circumstances are identifiably unique, concern with peer practice may be irrelevant.

At some point the time for fact-gathering and analyzing comes to an end. When I believe I have all the pieces in front of me I begin to cogitate. I start with the current equity-fixed allocation. I then weigh various factors I have discussed plus a few others. I come up with an alternative policy only to challenge it. I get someone whose opinion I respect to argue with me about what is best for the investor. I proceed like this until I have the best result I can fashion judgmentally. I am looking for just two numbers, like 60 and 40. That's it.

Once the risk policy is established, I advocate heavy indexing of investments. I strongly discourage closet indexing. Whether or not to invest in other types of assets, e.g., real estate, private equity or hedge funds, is a matter of taste and talent, and definitely a second-order consideration.

It is possible to invest institutional funds with greater efficiency. But doing so requires that we accept certain realities of investment markets, such as the fact that the stock market consistently beats investors rather than the other way around. In my work I have found that it also helps to place informed human judgment above purely quantitative forms of investment policy analysis. Give it a shot.

APPENDIX 2

Select *Financial Analysts Journal* Editorials

Big Bond Bust

Sep/Oct 2009, Vol. 65, No. 3: 6-8

With stocks, private equity, hedge funds, real estate and commodities losing 20–40 percent of their value in 2008, it was a great year for bond portfolios to fulfill their promise as investors' main source of downside protection. Investment-grade bonds did just that: The Barclays Capital Aggregate Bond Index returned 5.2 percent in 2008. A 35 percent portfolio allocation to assets earning a positive 5 percent return went a long way to blunt otherwise abysmal market returns. Alas, many investors did not enjoy that type of protection from their actively managed "core" and "core-plus" bond portfolios. Most core-plus portfolios actually lost money in 2008. A distressingly large number, including those of some prominent bond managers, suffered declines of up to 15 percent. Reflecting on the perplexing experience of 2008, a bewildered client asked, "When did our bond managers stop buying bonds?"

Bond portfolio management began to morph more than 25 years ago. Even back then, managers realized that if their portfolios were limited to the credit-rating restrictions of an investment-grade bond index, consistently beating the index net of fees would be difficult to do. And so began a long cycle of "enhancing" bond portfolios' return potential. It began innocuously enough with the inclusion of split-rated bonds, whereby one agency's rating met the cutoff for investment grade but that of another did not. Downgraded bonds were selectively retained. And the odd below-investment-grade bond was added to the portfolio with the client's approval.

From there, bond managers began seeking authorization to place a percentage of assets—say, up to 10–15 percent of the port-folio—in bonds with ratings one or two notches below the invest-ment-grade limit. As time passed, this and other variance percent-ages grew to as much as 40 percent of the total as emerging market debt, non-government-backed mortgage-related securities, and other types of assets that fell outside the benchmark became fair game.

The derivatives markets opened up new frontiers for creative risk taking. Now, some flagship bond funds encompass long and short exposures with notional values several times that of invested capital. Some funds sell protection via the credit default swap mar-ket. Some maintain thousands of complex positions. And some resemble leveraged fixed-income arbitrage hedge funds. When all is said and done, this is not your father's bond portfolio. Through it all, however, by convention, core-plus strategies have generally been benchmarked against investment-grade bond indices.

Most core-plus bond portfolios exceeded the return of the Barclays Capital Aggregate Bond Index with a fair degree of con-sistency in the years leading up to 2008. This performance reflected the collective payoff of numerous risks that had little to do with the coupon payments and yield-curve dynamics of the bonds that make up the index. But 2008 was a year of reckoning; as noted, after several years of steady, moderate gains, many of these funds experienced extreme losses. When the credit crunch finally hit, heavy reliance on credit securities was a big part of the problem. As is typically the case when credit markets are stressed, flight-to-quality liquidations became an important dynamic that put downward pressure even on bonds of solvent issuers. Fixed-income-arbitrage positions often have subtle, complex liquidity characteristics of their own. Thus, acute liquidity effects exacerbated the losses of many aggressive strategies.

The high-octane bond strategy is reminiscent of what Andrew Lo describes in "Risk Management for Hedge Funds."[1] Lo illustrates the performance of a hypothetical hedge fund, Capital Decimation Partners, that produces steady profits for many years by selling deep out-of-the-money put options, only to have its day of reckoning. Referring to the strategy's asymmetric payoff pattern, Lo notes, "This is a very specific type of risk signature that is not well summarized by static measures such as standard deviation" (p. 23). And so it is with core-plus bond management.

For the 10 years ended 30 June 2009, the average return of 94 core-plus bond funds in the eVestment Alliance eASE Database was 6.09 percent before fees. (That figure reflects the inevitable upward bias associated with self-reporting and survivorship.) Over the same period, the average return of the Barclays Capital Aggregate Bond Index was 5.98 percent. The average fee for accounts of $25 million is 37 bps, which places the average net performance differential at −26 bps. One would think that this record would dim considerably the luster of core-plus.

Is this editorial yet another tirade on the diseconomy of active investment for most investors? To be sure, it is not. Rather, I call into question the suitability of such investment techniques for that part of the investor's portfolio that bears the brunt of providing downside protection. In 2008, we were reminded that presumed moderate correlation of risky assets is an unreliable source of downside protection in extreme market conditions. Once again, we realized that genuine and reliably high-quality fixed-income investments constitute the one and only true bulwark against loss in growth-oriented portfolios.

If old-fashioned bonds belong in the bond portfolio to preserve its integrity, where should advanced, aggressive fixed-income strategies be allowed to come to full flower? In my last editorial, I proposed a simple approach to asset allocation that uses three "buckets."[2] Bucket One is for downside protection and comprises investment-grade fixed income that is structured to reflect the investor's unique circumstances and managed passively (cheaply). Bucket Two comprises global stock index funds to capture the equity risk premium and provide growth (cheaply). Bucket Three is for all manner of superior active strategies, regardless of asset class or style. Bucket Three would be the logical place for high-octane fixed-income strategies to reside in this three-bucket model.

In a more conventional asset allocation framework, let us assume that the bond allocation of an investor's policy is executed via a conservative, low-cost investment-grade bond portfolio. Value-added fixed-income strategies could be "equitized" or made market neutral with derivatives and reside with active equity and/or hedge fund strategies. This approach would be a sensible way to classify and corral these strategies.

Nor is this editorial a condemnation of the extraordinary advances in investment management brought about by the innovation of our fixed-income-management colleagues. At its best, state-of-the-art fixed-income management is a remarkable demonstration of the advances in financial engineering. Bravo! But under the best of circumstances, two problems remain. Comparing core-plus bond portfolio results with those of an investment-grade index like the Barclays flies in the face of our performance measurement precepts: You don't run greyhounds on steroids against a slow rabbit. The other problem is more profound: Aggressive, unpredictable, active-investment strategies should not be allowed to undermine the essential character of an investor's principal source of downside protection.

Darwin and Investment Product Proliferation

The following is adapted from the essay, "The Structure of the Investment Management Industry," appearing in *Financial Analysts Journal*, July/August 1997, Vol. 53, No. 4:6-13

By any measure recent growth in the number of investment products has been astonishing. For example, Nelson Publications (Port Chester, New York), which reports on products for tax-exempt investors, identified approximately 9,000 products in 1996, up from 6,600 as recently as 1993. Hedge funds, which were relatively uncommon not long ago, now number approximately 4,700 (Van Hedge Fund Advisors, Nashville, Tennessee). The trend toward multi-product firms is discerned most readily in the mutual fund industry, for which data are available on the number of managers as well as products. Between 1985 and 1995, the number of mutual fund managers more than doubled (increasing from 252 to 558) and the number of funds increased from 1,528 to 5,761.[3] Even allowing for the growth in the number of fund managers, the number of funds offered per manager increased from an average of 6 to 10.

What accounts for product proliferation in an industry that has struggled to deliver on the implied promise of its products? A parallel in the field of natural selection does, in fact, provide the key to understanding an industry transformation that has been underway for more than a decade.

Adaptation

Biologists distinguish between two adaptive strategies—*r* and K—that species use in reproduction. The *r* strategy is prevalent in a challenging environment in which resources are scarce and risks are great. The K strategy prevails when the environment favors a particular species and, in terms of gene transmission, parents' life resources are more productively applied in protecting and nurturing offspring than in further reproduction. The pure r strategy involves bearing large numbers (even millions) of offspring with no parental investment. Offspring survive largely through chance. The pure K strategy involves bearing very few, high-quality offspring during a lifetime, with substantial parental investment. Most species combine the two strategies to some extent. Inasmuch as each organism has finite life resources to expend in reproduction, an optimal trade-off of r and K exists for each species in a given environment. Species often change strategies to adapt; unable to do so, some become extinct.

Evolution of Investment Management

These *life-history adaptations*, as they are known to biologists, have an analog in the evolution of investment management. In the investment-management industry, product development is analogous to procreation; investing in a product is analogous to nurturing offspring. Finite capital requires trading off product investment for product development within individual firms. To the extent that investment markets are efficient, the environment for active investment products is challenging. That is, owing to management and custody fees and trading costs, the expected value added by these products is collectively negative, which makes long-run client satisfaction problematic. The more efficient the market, the more challenging the environment—and the more product survival relies on chance.

During the past 25 years, a gradual shift has occurred in the allocation of resources in the investment-management industry. In days gone by, investment firms typically invested heavily in a single product, the investment often taking the form of a large securities analysis staff. With the passage of time, many management firms came to realize that consistently beating the market is hard to do—and risky in terms of longevity—with only one product to carry the firm. Also during this period, marketing and client-service executives were on the rise in the business, and many firms began to place greater emphasis on product development and marketing. The era and art of product development and marketing came into full flower 10–15 years ago, and product proliferation began in earnest. Fifteen years ago, for firms to have more than a few products was uncommon, and most had only one; now, having a half-dozen or more is not uncommon.

In effect, some one-product firms concluded that trying to beat the market was not a particularly good business; they discovered that there is too much randomness to make reliance on a single product pay off with a high degree of confidence. For these firms, product development and marketing became at least as important as beating the market. That realization, in my judgment, accounts for much of the product proliferation we observe today, which is the equivalent of an adaptive shift from K to r. In competitive markets, as in nature, survival is linked to adaptability. Active product development is an appropriate adaptive response if managers perceive the markets in which they trade to be efficient.

Can you think of a manager that has not only survived but flourished over several decades managing a single portfolio? I can think of only one: Berkshire Hathaway.

The Uncorrelated Return Myth

May/June 2009, Vol. 65, No. 3:6-10

We have rituals at my house. Every fall, for example, my wife reminds me that it is time to clean out the basement. I generally accomplish this task by moving as much of my junk as I can to the attic. And every spring, she points out that it is time to clean out the attic, at which time I manage to relocate most of the relics to a familiar spot in the basement. After 34 years of this routine, I finally confronted the facts: If it has no value or constitutes a hazard, I should get rid of it. So, this fall I tracked down the local junk dealer and had him remove what should have been discarded long ago.

This seasonal ritual got me thinking that the investment profession should clean house from time to time. Events of the last year have shown us that a prime opportunity exists to do just that in the field of asset allocation.

For the last several years, the Holy Grail of asset allocation has been assets that offer "uncorrelated return." The premise is that assets with equity-like risk premiums are, for all intents and purposes, uncorrelated with the broad market. Availing themselves amply of such assets, investors can create high-returning, comparatively low-risk portfolios because they get the average of the risk premiums but the risk itself largely cancels out. Or so the story goes.

We should test propositions like "uncorrelated return" in two ways. First, we should evaluate them critically in light of accepted theory. Second, we should test them empirically. As a result of this two-pronged approach, we may revise theory. But if a proposition contradicts established theory and is disputed by the evidence, it should be discarded.

Theory

A cornerstone of asset-pricing theory is that investors may expect to be compensated for risk they cannot diversify away. Diversification is essentially a costless activity, so one has no reason to expect to be paid for a risk one can dissipate for naught.

For example, take the capital asset pricing model (CAPM). It posits that an asset's expected risk premium is proportional to its market sensitivity, or beta coefficient. What is a beta coefficient? It breaks down to the ratio of the standard deviation of the asset's risk premium to that of the market, multiplied by the correlation coefficient between the asset and the market. Thus, beta (and expected risk premium) is directly related to the relative riskiness of the asset and the correlation of the asset's return with that of the market. Therefore, no "uncorrelated assets" with positive risk premiums can exist because the market accords a risk premium only to market-correlated assets.

Although CAPM has been a source of controversy for nearly a half century, it remains the leading theory of asset pricing. More important, however, even though scholars challenge CAPM, rarely do they attack a critical proposition that underlies it: namely, that one cannot expect to get paid for a risk that can be eliminated without cost. This principle is a bedrock of asset-pricing theory.

Evidence

Popular assets for inclusion under the heading "uncorrelated return" are real estate, hedge funds, and private equity. Table 1 reports the correlation of return of these assets with the S&P 500

Index over the 36 months ended 30 September 2009. In all cases, the proxy for the asset class is based on returns generated daily in an auction market.[4] Table 1 reveals a high degree of correlation between these assets and the stock market.

Table 1
Correlation of Return of Assets with the S&P 500
1 October 2006– 30 September 2009

Asset	Correlation with S&P 500
Real Estate	0.81
Hedge Funds	0.66
Private Equity	0.84

The correlation of hedge funds with stocks is undoubtedly understated by virtue of the stale pricing that characterizes that asset class.[5] Some of the other asset classes, such as real estate and private equity, give the illusion that they are largely uncorrelated with the stock market because they use appraisals or accounting definitions of value (e.g., net asset value) in establishing the infrequent valuations that go into the calculation of returns. But sticky valuations should not be mistaken for the absence of common economic dependence on forces that move market prices. Many learned this lesson painfully in 2008.

None of the foregoing is meant to imply that these assets do not belong in diversified portfolios. To be sure, they can improve portfolio efficiency. But there is no free lunch in asset allocation: If you hope to collect the risk premium, you must bear the risk.

The notion of the existence of "uncorrelated return" assets with handsome risk premiums flies in the face of financial theory and conflicts with empirical evidence. So, reject it we must. Accordingly, on behalf of self-respecting investment professionals everywhere, I hereby consign the shibboleth of "uncorrelated return" to the scrap heap of asset allocation lingo, where it shall be available only to unscrupulous sellers, credulous buyers, and unschooled investment analysts.

Parsimonious Asset Allocation
May/June 2009, Vol. 65, No. 3:6-10

Several years ago, I challenged the reigning "style-box" approach to diversification of stock portfolios:

The conventional architecture for managing a large pension fund's domestic equity portfolio is to divide it among several managers with complementary investment styles, with "style" increasingly defined as emphasizing stocks of a type, such as growth or value, small- or large-capitalization. The pension fund client ordinarily allocates assets among predominantly long-only specialists so that aggregate characteristics of the portfolio resemble those of a particular stock market benchmark, e.g., the Wilshire 5000 or Russell 3000 stock index. Large pension funds employ an average of 8.7 active equity managers; one in four employs ten or more.... .

... Clients and consultants labor to piece these fragmentary portfolios together into a superior whole in a manner that brings to mind assembling a jigsaw puzzle. They are not qualified to make dynamic, relative-value judgments among market sectors or manager styles, so they are left to attempt to enforce a certain style purity among managers, keeping each in its designated style "box," and plugging gaps between boxes in an effort to maintain a so-called style-neutral portfolio. Consequently, rigid and rather arbitrary boundaries develop within the client's portfolio.... Portfolios of this architecture have underperformed by the margin of their cost, making closet indexing an apt characterization.[6]

Reliance on the pigeonhole approach to manager diversification has declined in recent years, which is good. Now is the time to apply Occam's razor to an even more important investment policy problem: overall asset allocation.

Categoryitis

One problem with state-of-the-art classification schemes is category proliferation. Some schemes use as many as 10 categories of investment, including developed market equity (domestic and foreign), emerging market equity, multiple classes of private equity, commodities, real estate, investment-grade bonds, high-yield bonds, and emerging market debt. A computer can generate countless combinations of all these categories. But can the typical investment committee member evaluate the results of such an exercise with anything resembling firsthand knowledge? Or must she simply accept, as an article of faith, an allocation scheme advanced by staff or consultant? Contemporary asset allocation schemes are becoming unwieldy for many decision makers if for no other reason than the proliferation and splintering of investment categories.

Another problem is the ambiguity of some categories. In addition to the asset classes previously described, several vague catch-all categories have become part of the mix. The popular category "alternatives"—which can include such disparate investments as private equity, hedge funds, and commodities—admits of so many possibilities that it might as well be called "miscellaneous" as far as risk–return particulars are concerned. Even the narrower category "hedge funds" does not so much constitute an asset class as describe a liberal approach to active investment that takes many forms. "Real assets" does have a compelling ring; all investors worry about inflation. But empirical support for the proposition that such assets as real estate, commodities, and timber are reliable inflation hedges is extremely weak. Does this fact mean that so-called real-asset investing is based more on gut instinct than on hard evidence? On more than one occasion, I have come across the category "risk reducers" or some such, which includes credit securities and "low-volatility" hedge funds. Call me old-fashioned, but this one strikes a particularly dissonant chord in me, especially after 2008. Nevertheless, it is fair—and important—to say that such ambiguous categories as the foregoing frustrate risk control, which is the primary goal of asset allocation.

The problem with contemporary asset categories is twofold: The number of categories is growing, and categories are becoming fuzzier. Reflecting on this situation, one is reminded of William of Occam's admonition that "entities should not be multiplied unnecessarily."

Faulty Assumptions

Over the last 25 years, institutional investors have become increasingly reliant on asset allocation models that use a complex set of assumptions about the future. Fixed-income allocations have steadily declined over the years among all types of investors as they have relied more and more on correlation forecasts to provide the basis of portfolio risk control. In 2008, the assumption of largely uncorrelated returns among stocks, hedge funds, commodities, private equity, and real estate broke down utterly. As a result, institutional investors of all types experienced losses far greater than the "worst-case" outcomes predicted by their asset allocation models. To be sure, volatility was greater than anticipated for some assets. But assumptions about the correlation of returns among asset classes were the real culprit.

It is important to recognize that over time, asset-class return correlations are unstable—really unstable. Consider the correlation of two of the most clearly defined and efficiently priced asset classes: large-cap U.S. stocks and investment-grade bonds. From 1994 to 2008, the 36-month correlation of this pair of assets meandered between 0.60 and −0.40. The instability of correlation coefficients isn't the only problem. Correlations involving hedge funds are subject to well-documented downward bias associated with stale pricing. The invariably low correlations ascribed to pairs involving private-market assets are virtually meaningless and seriously misleading. And yet, institutional investors regularly bet their bundles on a pack of correlation coefficients.

Some would say that 2008 was an exceptional year. Indeed it was, but by no means was it unique. We witnessed global meltdowns in 1987 and in 1998. Globally integrated markets, the pervasive use of derivatives, and our herding nature ensure that we will experience more of the same in the future. All of which raises the question, What good is a system of risk control that fails when you need it most?

Parsimony in Asset Allocation

Although I cannot posit a fully formed parsimonious asset allocation model in this limited space, I can sketch the broad outlines of one. By "parsimonious" asset allocation, I mean an approach that relies primarily on self-evident truths and hard empirical evidence rather than on assumptions or intuition. I also mean one that uses a minimal number of clearly defined categories. To describe this model, I begin with the question, what do investors want?

Investors want three things. They want some downside protection. They want to capture the equity risk premium to the maximum extent consistent with their preference for downside protection. And most would also like to garner excess return (alpha), although we know that, by definition, only about half do so over any particular span of time.

Consider this three-asset-class model: (1) both nominal- and real-pay U.S. Treasury securities of varying maturities, (2) a global stock index fund, and (3) an active component. The logic is equally simple: Default-free bonds provide risk control. A global stock index fund cleanly captures the equity risk premium. The active portfolio is an omnibus category that incorporates the most compelling opportunities available to the investor for exploiting market inefficiency and capturing liquidity premiums.

The Bond Portfolio

Reckoning the need for reliable fixed-income investments should be the starting point of every investment policy review. Will cash be needed soon? Are there any dollar-and-date-specific liabilities (nominal or real) we should hedge? Do we want a reliable way to mitigate market risk? A structured, default-risk-free bond portfolio meets these requirements at very low cost to the investor.

The Stock Index Fund

Capturing the equity risk premium, to the extent consistent with one's tolerance for risk, is of prime interest to most investors. The most reliable and inexpensive way to capture the equity risk premium is by means of a global index fund. Any investor can secure the return of a portfolio of more than 6,000 common stocks across nearly 50 country markets. Investing passively guarantees that the investor will capture the equity risk premium.

The Active Portfolio

The active portfolio comprises all the attractive investment opportunities an investor can identify and access. These opportunities might be skilled hedge fund or long-only managers—managers who work in a single asset class (or in a niche within one) or multi-asset-class managers. They might include private equity or real estate investments or transitory credit-dislocation strategies. Put simply, these investment opportunities are carefully researched and attractive. But each opportunity must possess its own idiosyncratic merit without regard to category.

Looking for investment opportunities is likely to be a fluid process inasmuch as they are often episodic. An investor may examine 100 opportunities a year but invest in no more than 15–20 at any one time. Relatively little emphasis would be placed on piecing the opportunities together to craft a particular set of factor exposures. The active portfolio is all about locating investment opportunities. Risk control is accomplished by diversifying among several active strategies and by means of bond and index fund investments.

Conclusion

Unanswered is the question of how one arrives at the proportions of assets allocated to each of the three segments. Although addressing this question thoroughly is beyond the scope of this commentary, it can be answered here briefly. The problem of allocation involves reconciling two dynamics: (1) the desired degree of downside protection and (2) the degree of investor confidence in the ability to identify superior strategies. In somewhat different words, it comes down to answering two questions asked in the right order: How big must the bond portfolio be so that we can sleep at night? How great is our confidence in our ability to pick winners?

A final question is, How should we evaluate this or any other asset allocation framework? I propose three tests: Does it provide a reliable way to limit market risk? Does it provide a reliable way to capture the equity risk premium? Does it permit implementation of creative active investment strategies without impediment? This parsimonious asset allocation model passes with flying colors and does so at minimal cost and without the investment committee's losing sight of the forest for the trees. Even old Occam might have liked it.

The Herd Follows the Leader
March/April 2008 Vol. 64, No. 2:6–8

In the Editor's Corner of July/August 2007, we briefly discussed the herding tendencies of institutional investors and noted similarities in investment policy among members of various classes of institutional investor, such as educational endowment funds and public pension funds. We raised a number of questions, including, If a class of funds occupies a distinct investment policy habitat irrespective of differences in circumstance among the funds, what accounts for the selection of habitat? In other words, how does the herd determine where to locate itself?

In this Editor's Corner, we want to address the tendency of the different members of one particular class of investors—educational endowment funds—to pursue the same or similar investment policies. We argue that competition drives them to do so.

Institutions of higher education are intense competitors. They compete for students, faculty, grants, private gifts, and ultimately, standing. Evidence of competition is writ large and small. At the macro level, each year, a frenzied ritual plays out across the United States. It brings college-bound high school seniors together with colleges and universities competing to fill out their freshman classes with the best students they can get. At the micro level, we recently saw competition play out between two top Ivy League schools. In December 2007, Harvard University announced that it would increase endowment spending to enable it to provide scholarships to students with family income as high as $180,000 a year. Harvard did this because it could: Its wealth has mushroomed. An indication of increased wealth is that the percentage of the endowment going to operations has declined from 5.1 percent to 4.3 percent in recent years. (Annual Financial Report of Harvard University, 2007) In effect, Harvard upped the ante for its competitors to play by using its extraordinary wealth to lower prices in the form of offering greater tuition discounts. Within a month, Yale University followed suit. Yale was able to do so because it, too, has experienced exceptional endowment growth. In discounting tuition in this way, Harvard and Yale played to their competitive strengths in a way that will allow them to be increasingly selective in rounding out future freshman classes.

Make no mistake, all institutions would like to maximize the growth of their endowment through superior investment gain. But some are better equipped to do so than others, and those that are so blessed tend to become the investment leaders. The leaders are rich in absolute and relative (endowment-per-student) terms. Also, they are often able to bring into play the uncommon investment expertise of alumni and trustees. These institutions, by virtue of being heavily endowed, have the financial wherewithal to sustain investments in equities and less liquid market sectors through difficult periods. They have the budgetary resources to assemble top-notch in-house investment operations. And their alumni and boards invariably include sophisticated investors who support and sometimes even guide the institution in being an early adopter of profitable new investment strategies.

Where, investment-wise, have these competitive advantages taken the leaders? Away from traditional investment policy: Fixed income typically represents 15 percent or less of these organizations' portfolio investments. U.S. equities no longer dominate the portfolios. Alternative investments, such as private equity, hedge funds, and commodities, account for up to half of the portfolios.

And there is little evidence of wasteful closet indexing, which characterizes some other sectors of institutional investing.

What do the endowment elites have to show for their nontraditional approach? Several, with Harvard and Yale prominent among them, have achieved exceptional track records over the past 15 years, earning returns well in excess of the average of smaller endowments, foundations, and the typical pension fund—public or private.

What about the less advantaged institutions that compete, directly or indirectly, with the investment leaders for students, faculty, and so on? If they stay with traditional investment policies, they risk seeing the wealth gap widen. So, one response is to emulate the leaders, which is what many educational endowments have been doing in recent years, even though most lack the advantages that enabled the leaders to set their course in these new directions. In short, the less advantaged from a competitive standpoint feel pressure to play the game of the advantaged. That is how competition often works— and how competition shapes, to a large extent, the investment habitat of educational endowments.

Is following the leaders right for everyone? Might some institutions find themselves playing over their heads, as it were? These are questions for another time.

Pensions or Penury?
January/February 2007, Vol. 63, No. 1:6

Pensions are the focus of this issue, which includes descriptions of the problems confronting defined-benefit and defined-contribution plans and thoughtful, creative solutions to the problems.

Even though people are living longer, they are saving less. And the reason is not that employers have been fattening pensions; they have not. What employers have been doing is shifting pension risk to workers—in ways straightforward (introducing defined-contribution plans) and not (using hopeful earnings assumptions in funding defined-benefit plans while relying more heavily on equity investments). In the United States, the venerable Social Security system is living on borrowed time.

This is not a pretty picture.

For this reason, we devote this issue to the challenge of producing retirement income. Barton Waring and Laurence Siegel aver that the defined-benefit (DB) plan is inherently superior to the defined-contribution (DC) alternative and an institution well worth preserving. They believe the key to doing so lies in acknowledging the financial character of pension claims and managing DB plans accordingly. In a similar spirit, Bernard Dumas and Juerg Syz propose trading pension claims, which would provide price discovery of pension liabilities for valuation purposes and enable beneficiaries to diversify the idiosyncratic credit risk of plan sponsors.

Martin Leibowitz and Anthony Bova conjecture that P/Es may decline under significantly lower as well as significantly higher real interest rates. They warn that under falling real rates, pensions defined in real terms could experience a sharp drop in funded ratios as a result of declining asset values and rising liabilities—the double whammy of pension finance.

Don Ezra succinctly summarizes what went wrong with DB plans, what he thinks future DB plans might look like, and how he sees DC plans being made to work better. He also reminds us that even with the best-engineered retirement income schemes, in planning for retirement, everyone faces profound personal choices: how much to save, how to invest, when to retire.

Keith Ambachtsheer offers a sweeping prescription for curing what he describes as a "sick" DB system. He eschews employer-based DB plans and conventional DC plans as seriously flawed. He proposes stand-alone TIAA-CREF–like institutions, such as those evolving in Australia and the Netherlands, as the way of the future. Hallmarks of his Utopian system include various "autopilot" mechanisms, such as mandatory participation, life-cycle investing, and gradually annuitizing investment balances.

Ralph Goldsticker offers a thought-provoking proposal: Revive the 17th century tontine as a cost-effective alternative to annuities. This risk-pooling device could be coupled with DC or cash-balance plans and offers the potential to increase pensions significantly.

Lawrence Bader and Jeremy Gold make the case against holding stock in public pension funds. They believe that, in addition to making pensions more secure, bond-only investment is more likely than stock/bond investment to produce intergenerational equity among taxpayers and is a better after-tax strategy for them. João Cocco and Paolo Volpin address a related theme in the context of private-sector U.K. plans. They provide empirical evidence of agency issues when corporate executives control pension funds, thus reviving concern over the existence of the "pension put" Jack Treynor identified 30 years ago.

If our collective conscience could speak to us, it would probably sound a lot like Charley Ellis. He believes the U.S. profession could have taken greater initiative in advocating legislation to enable DC plans to work better. Ellis exhorts us now to exert influence on DC plan sponsors to adopt automatic enrollment and promote participant education and the use of life-cycle investment options.

Investment Policy: Bridle of Want

March/April 2007, Vol. 63, No. 2:8

Investors everywhere are stretching for return. Pension funds strain to meet return assumptions that exceed proper liability discount rates by hundreds of basis points. Endowed institutions strive to earn superior returns even as they become richer. Assets have poured into leveraged buyout funds at an unprecedented rate. And many investors have taken the prospect of earning "mere" single-digit returns as an injunction to incur non-market risk in the hope of "adding alpha." In short, investment thinking today appears to be heavily influenced by want.

Is anything wrong with this attitude? After all, economics tells us that it is rational to prefer more wealth than what we have now. Indeed, preferring greater wealth is what motivates investors to assume risk. If people did not want more, there would be no risk capital, no enterprise, no economic growth.

But successful investment requires more than motivation. It also requires direction and control, which are the functions of investment policy. Investors motivated by want but lacking a well-thought-out investment policy can find themselves, in fact, incurring more risk or illiquidity than suits them. Or wasting precious resources trying to exploit security mispricing (garner alpha) in highly efficient markets.

Investment policy has three dimensions, all grounded in investor capacity—not want, preference, or ambition. One is the capacity to bear risk. The second is the capacity to hold illiquid assets. The third is the capacity to exploit security mis- pricing. Investment policy also must be shaped by market realities and, in particular, by logical return expectations.

Investors with little or no tolerance for risk typically earn a return not unlike the rate of inflation, which means they can generally expect to preserve the purchasing power of their wealth. Those that can live with stock market volatility can expect—in the usual economic sense, which involves uncertainty—a greater return. Investors with an even greater risk tolerance combined with the ability to part with funds for several years can prudently invest in private equity. Private equity offers a high expected return to compensate investors for the liquidity they are willing to surrender as well as the greater risk they are willing to bear. Thus, sensible investors learn to reconcile their desire for building wealth with their capacity to tolerate risk and illiquidity.

As for adding return through active management, that opportunity belongs to investors with the ability, not simply the desire, to do so. This group includes skillful money managers and those investors able to identify and use those managers at a reasonable price. And those with skill will exploit it whenever they can, not just when nominal rates are relatively low.

So, although a preference for greater wealth motivates us to consider taking investment risk and to evaluate alternative investment strategies, it is insufficient to inform investment policy. Sound investment policy requires that we regularly and carefully evaluate our circumstances to determine our tolerance for loss and our liquidity requirements. It also requires that we make a sober assessment of our ability to beat the market consistently, net of costs. In mapping out investment strategy, these are the issues that warrant our attention and energy—especially when we are tempted to stretch for return.

New Organizational Paradigm:
A Portfolio Manager and a Band of Scouts

July/August 2008, Vol. 64, No. 4:8-10

Hedge funds and a few pioneers in the traditional investment management business began altering the nature of investment management in the 1980s. The traditional approach involved trying to eke out a little extra return from diversified, often narrowly stylized, long-only portfolios. The upstarts eschewed this approach in the interest of capturing alpha however they could. If they had to cross traditional asset-class boundaries, make extensive use of derivatives, sell short, and introduce some leverage, so be it.

Widespread efforts to separate alpha and beta, as we say, are having another effect. They have begun to alter the way institutional investors organize their key resource—that is, their human talent.

Traditional Staff Organization

Traditionally, the organization of the professional staff of a large institutional portfolio was along asset-class lines, with an investment team handling each component of the target asset allocation of the total fund. The asset-class approach to organization was a mainstay for three decades. Usually, each asset-class team managed a "perfect portfolio," by which I mean one with its own benchmark, strategic allocation to passive and active management, blend of management styles, and allowable tracking error. The goal was to produce a portfolio with meticulous risk control, as if each asset class were a whole portfolio unto itself. Management of the total fund often amounted to little more than rolling up the asset-class portfolios accounting-wise at the end of each reporting period.

Frequently, the unit for each asset class employed many so-called portfolio managers, internally and externally. So decentralized was the approach that even very large funds could operate with little central investment staff and, in some cases, without even a designated chief investment officer (CIO).

New investment strategies have caused large investors to rethink organization. Some strategies straddle asset classes; an example is those that use derivatives to get beta exposure in one asset class and actively manage direct investments in another. When investment opportunity moves among asset classes as freely as within them, the traditional organization inhibits active risk exposures from crossing asset-class boundaries, so it is a hindrance. And we see a growing appreciation in the modern era that porting beta easily and cheaply is critical, but it is difficult to do when strict organizational boundaries hamper such a creative dynamic.

A New Organizational Paradigm

A few years ago, I began advocating a new organizational paradigm, one that is functional rather than asset-class oriented. The new paradigm calls for two principal boxes on the organization chart beneath that of the CIO. One box is labeled Portfolio Management, and the other, Scouts. (For the purpose of this discussion, I am ignoring private- market assets, such as real estate and private equity. You can think of them, as well as internally managed active portfolios, as additional boxes under the CIO.)

Functions of Portfolio Management, all of which occur at the total fund level, are as follows:

- investment policy analysis leading to the establishment of a fund's target asset allocation,
- risk analytics and performance attribution,

- beta management, by way of index funds, exchange-traded funds, and/or derivatives,
- the control of active risk,
- rebalancing—strategy and execution—and
- transition management.

In short, the Portfolio Management unit controls beta exposures and active risk at the total fund level. It is not engaged directly in efforts to exploit security mispricing; rather, it implements decisions made elsewhere and controls risk. This new organization contains only one portfolio manager; it is a unit comprising several people with considerable technical expertise working on a single portfolio.

The function of Scouts is just as you would expect: to seek exceptional active management opportunity wherever it may lie. They are talent scouts, looking for investment managers that have a distinct edge and doing so without regard to asset class or style. Conceivably, they could even identify exceptional managers whose areas of expertise fall beyond the fund's target asset allocation, which the investor could exploit as long as Portfolio Management has a way to hedge any unwanted factor exposure. In my work with large investors, I have found that evaluating diverse active strategies head-to-head forces one to think hard about the nature of each manager's edge, inasmuch as the alternatives are not otherwise comparable.

Scouts search for manager talent and vet candidates continuously. They recommend firms for retention. They monitor retained managers and recommend termination and allocation shifts. Scouts are likely to be the "gray hairs" in the organization because extensive and varied experience with active management is critical in their work. Yet, the scouts control no assets.

In the new organization, the CIO approves active strategies. And it is the CIO, often with the help of a committee of senior colleagues, who determines the distribution of active risk among strategies—determining the relative magnitude of the bets, as it were, within the active risk budget established by the oversight board.

Benefits and Challenges

Large investors gain three benefits from functional organization:

- Increased flexibility and decreased friction in securing active and passive exposures,
- Keen attention to what constitutes a manager's edge when considerations of manager type and style largely evaporate in the manager evaluation process, and
- Decreased probability of closet indexing because only one portfolio is being managed and active bets across the portfolio can be summarized numerically on a single page.

The modern organization requires new tools and talents. It must master risk analytics of a more universal nature than in the past (i.e., ones that transcend asset-class boundaries). Indeed, superior portfolio risk modeling is the sine qua non of the new paradigm. Also, trading capabilities must be geared to the requirement of deftly managing beta exposures at minimum cost.

Perhaps, the biggest challenge in moving to the new paradigm is cultural. In the traditional organization, decentralization was maximized; various units and individuals within the units "owned" parts of the portfolio and operated the parts "locally." The new approach involves an altogether different division of labor.

Evolution, Not Revolution

Migration from the traditional asset-class organization ion to a functional organization is invariably gradual. In some cases, organizations are not even consciously aware of it. Nevertheless, signs of transformation are evident. Large investors are

- developing risk analytics that work across asset classes and experimenting with active-risk budgeting,
- allocating more and more resources to central portfolio management activities,
- attempting to lessen the separation between asset-class teams,
- hiring managers with strategies that don't fit neatly into traditional style grids, and
- hiring globally oriented managers that, by their nature, bridge asset classes.

Employing a large staff to manage a fund's marketable securities signals a commitment to beating the market because even large-scale and complex passive investment is feasible with a very small staff. Yet, beating the market has proved to be elusive for most investors. The new organizational paradigm is one way to improve the odds of success.

End of an Era
January/February 2009, Vol. 65, No. 1:6-8.

Profits on the exchange are the treasures of goblins. At one time they may be carbuncle stones, then coals, then diamonds, then flint stones, then morning dew, then tears.

—Félix Lope de Vega, 1562–1635

We are witnessing the end of an era.

It was an era born of economic malaise: the stagflation of the 1970s and recessions of the early 1980s. At its dawning, you could pick up U.S. Treasuries yielding 13 percent and stocks at single-digit price-to-earnings ratios. Risk—not the prospect of market gains or garnering "alpha"—weighed heavily on investors' minds in the beginning.

The era got off to a rousing start, with U.S. stocks soaring 65 percent in the first year after the market bottomed out in August 1982.

It was an era marked by vigorous global competition from the outset. Early on, Japan, with its manufacturing prowess, corporate wealth, and powerful banking resources, appeared poised to become the dominant economic power. The Japanese threat roused a torpid U.S. economy, and intense global competition—globalization, as it came to be known—began in earnest. It was one of the most productive periods in modern economic history. The fall of the Berlin Wall provided the fillip that enabled the economic revolution to spread to Eastern Europe, Russia, and even China. India, the sleeping giant, came to life. As Thomas Friedman observed, the world became flat.

From the beginning of the era, leveraged finance was the mother's milk of expansion. Michael Milken, "the Junk Bond King," fueled the growth of takeovers and bankrolled early leveraged buyout specialist Kohlberg Kravis Roberts & Company. Buying on credit became the financial hallmark of the era.

Stocks rose briskly through the 1980s. In October 1987, markets finally stumbled, losing nearly a quarter of their value in a single day. But investors largely took it in stride. Wealth had been amassed so quickly that few had gotten used to thinking of it as *their* money; rather, there was a pervasive sense among investors at the time that they had been playing with the house's money. And it took a mere 19 months to fully recover the loss and for the market to begin establishing new highs.

On the eve of the 1990s, reflecting on the extraordinary gains of the 1980s, one thoughtful observer remarked that only one thing was sure to be true of investing in the 1990s: Stock market gains, if any, would be modest in comparison with what we had witnessed in the 1980s. And then it got interesting.

Stock prices continued their steady ascent through the middle of the 1990s, and then, they really took off. The dot-com–media–telecom bubble was born. The accretion of wealth, combined with foolishly easy credit, spawned a separate bubble in housing prices. Between 1997 and 2004 in the United States, housing prices rose by more than 50 percent. Even the demise of the tech frenzy did nothing to arrest the positive momentum in housing prices.

It was an era in which pioneering efforts in a handful of university investment offices began to reinvent portfolio management, and the "endowment model" was born. Some investment offices produced sustained, extraordinary gains through canny diversification and astute manager selection. These investors were bona fide champions of the era. But this success story had a downside: It inspired large numbers of ordinary investors to channel great sums into anything "alternative" on the basis of little more than an encouraging, albeit misleading, historical covariance matrix.

Not surprisingly, the emulators turned to the endowment model. Imitating Warren Buffett had become impractical after the mid-1990s; by then, cheap stocks were in scarce supply. So, instead of buying assets that offered old-fashioned risk premiums, many investors pinned their hopes on the wonders—and the myth—of "uncorrelated returns."

In the era just ended, hedge funds flourished in spite of their implausible compensation arrangements. Some exceptional investment talent found its way to that sector, to be sure. But more than anything else, a single, remarkable event propelled hedge funds above the trillion-dollar level of assets: Hedge funds played the bursting of the internet bubble just right, riding high-flying stocks up and bailing out near the top.

Just as leverage had played a key part throughout the era, it took on a starring role at the end. By the first few years of this century, oceans of liquidity were sloshing about in world markets. Liquidity of that scale, it seems, makes anything possible. Easy credit was everywhere, and leverage seeped into every nook and cranny of the world economy and financial markets. Perhaps the greatest shortcoming of regulators, financial institutions, and investment professionals was that we couldn't see it. We could feel it, like the ground trembling beneath our feet before an earthquake. But we couldn't frame it properly, let alone imagine the destructive force of the eruption that was to come.

With this issue of the Financial Analysts Journal, we inaugurate a series of articles that reflect on the era just ended and what might lie ahead. Titled "Global Financial Crisis," the series will address a wide range of topics, including internationally integrated markets, market regulation, market transparency, the structure of institutions, the nature of incentives, contagion and bubbles, behavioral economics, the perils of financial modeling, and some good old Graham-and-Dodd security analysis. An overarching theme will be putting to use what we have learned, because painfully reliving the past, over and over again, is a miserable way for civilization to move through time.

Hedge Fund Clones: Triumph of Form over Substance
May/June 2007, Vol. 63, No. 3:6-7

When I first heard about cloning hedge funds, I was reading Michael Crichton's latest novel *Next*, a bioengineering, sci-fi thriller. In one plot line, a biotech entrepreneur is hot on the trail of a gene that promotes resistance to cancer. The sole source of the gene is a fellow who has no intention of surrendering any of his body tissue— at least not without getting a big piece of the action. The greedy biotech executive thus dispatches a team of DNA bounty hunters equipped with a bottle of chloroform and long needles to get the goods, so to speak. So, the talk of cloning hedge funds caused me, in an admittedly credulous moment, to surmise that someone had uncovered genetic material belonging to Albert Winslow Jones and was hoping to reincarnate the prime mover. Or that George Soros was— quite literally—franchising himself in his golden years. Or that Michael Steinhardt, perhaps, was getting 2-and-20 for a few drops of blood. Soon, I discovered just how wrong I was.

Hedge fund cloning (or hedge fund replication, as it is also known) is an extension of efforts to develop models to explain hedge fund performance. Hedge fund performance evaluation is difficult because hedge funds lack stated benchmarks, often hedge their market exposures, and generally lack transparency. The benchmarking effort began with regressing hedge fund returns on a market index. This step quickly led to incorporating multiple market indexes and other return factors (e.g., credit and carry spreads) when it became apparent that various influences were at work.

Autocorrelation of hedge fund returns, indicative of illiquid holdings, was soon discovered, and some in the profession began to develop techniques to cope with it in evaluating performance. Then, observers noticed the prevalence of asymmetric return patterns, characteristic of option pricing–based trading strategies, and practitioners devised clever ways to model them. Although much work remains to be done, the profession has made important progress in developing performance metrics for hedge funds.

Hedge fund replication takes this knowledge a step further to create investment products that exhibit typical hedge fund return properties. These properties are the systematic components of a hedge fund's performance, just as the beta coefficient is the systematic component of a stock's return. And these systematic or beta-type elements have been shown to explain much of hedge fund return behavior.

The proponents of cloning cite as benefits of the clones liquidity, transparency, and above all, lower cost—no more 2-and-20. They claim that clones will do as well as or better than the real thing, if for no other reason than their lower cost.

Now that I understand what hedge fund clones are, what I don't understand is why anyone would want to invest in one.

The original attraction of hedge funds was their devotion to exploiting security mispricing and minimizing deadweight diversification. Hedge funds were to be the instruments of "pure alpha"—so unlike conventional, long-only portfolios, whose returns are primarily of the beta type. Alpha, of course, derives from market insights available to a select few. Such insights are proprietary and idiosyncratic—just the opposite of systematic.

Clones, in contrast, are entirely lacking in proprietary insight. They generate returns that are purely systematic, albeit often in a more complex manner than the way the capital asset pricing model prescribes the systematic component of stock returns. Thus, although hedge fund clones mimic the return behavior of a class of actual hedge funds, they have, by design, no alpha. They do, however, have an active management fee on the order of 1 percent of assets.

It's hard to know which is more off-putting: ultra-pricey hedge funds laden with common systematic risk exposures or clones that sidestep altogether the pesky problem of earning alpha while offering a "more reasonable" active fee than actual hedge funds charge. Paying active fees for passive products—no matter how elegant the products' design—is no way to win the investment game.

The Investment Policy Fizzle
July/August 2007, Vol. 63, No. 4:6-8.

Thirty-five years ago, I quit a perfectly good job as an up-and-coming institutional portfolio manager to take up investment consulting—investment policy consulting, to be specific. Having concluded I was insufficiently gifted to beat (or time) the market and unsure whether anyone truly was, I dedicated myself to the nascent field of helping institutional investors establish rational investment policies— ones appropriate to their circumstances and risk tolerance. If beating the market is unlikely, I reasoned determining how one ought to approach the market in terms of stock/bond/cash allocation would be the top priority of sophisticated investors.

It was a watershed time for this type of work. Quadratic portfolio optimization was just becoming computationally feasible. The landmark University of Chicago (Fisher and Lorie) study of historical stock returns provided the first empirical basis for estimates of future return and risk.[7] And the earliest applications of Monte Carlo simulation were used to map frequency distributions of potential future return for alternative asset allocation policies into distributions of a more concrete nature for investors to compare and evaluate.

Those were heady days for the investment policy pioneers. It was the dawning of an era, the launching of a quest to establish the logical basis of investment policy and to help investors identify optimal investment portfolios.

Alas, when we reflect fairly on the practice of devising institutional investment policy, accomplishments of the last 35 years appear rather meager.

Symptoms

On what do we base this assertion? Asset allocation models abound, to be sure. And most institutions dutifully conduct investment policy studies every three years or so. It is also true that no self-respecting institutional investor today would be without an investment policy statement. Yet, there are signs indicating that institutional investment policy development is an inchoate science.

Failure to integrate. The number one lesson of portfolio theory is that, because of the potential for sub-portfolio risks to offset one another, total portfolio is what matters. Yet, in deciding investment policy, institutional investors generally do not integrate the pension or endowment portfolio with the corporation's or institution's other assets and liabilities.

Fifteen years ago, Robert Merton outlined a method for integrating the investment policy of an educational endowment portfolio with the institution's other assets.[8] The concept is to devise a portfolio risk policy that is consonant with the institution's overall risk tolerance and the value and risk characteristics of its other assets, including the present value of future cash flows from various sources—e.g., tuition. In practice, it doesn't happen. In establishing an endowment investment policy, most colleges and universities give, at best, passing consideration to other assets and liabilities.

Fischer Black long ago described an optimal investment policy for corporate pension plans that integrates pension fund investment policy and corporate capital structure.[9] The strategy that maximizes the value of the firm is a bond-only pension portfolio.

Other frameworks exist for establishing comprehensive investment policy. In practice, however, they are all largely ignored.

Public pension funds in the United States regularly conduct asset/liability studies. And yet, there is no relationship between the funded status of public pension plans and their allocation to equities. On average, the most poorly funded state plans exhibit the same equity allocation as those that are exceptionally well funded. Moreover, attempts to integrate public pension fund investment policy more broadly with a state's finances are unheard of.

In short, institutional investors have generally failed to integrate portfolio investment policy into the larger context of the circumstances of the bearer of investment risk. Why? Why have ostensibly sophisticated and well-advised institutions not heeded the first lesson of portfolio theory and integrated their risk decisions?

Herding and the advisor effect. In the absence of integration, investment policy takes shape in other ways. The asset allocation of large public pension funds in the United States—besides being invariant with respect to funded status—is remarkably homogenous. The current norm is approximately 75 percent equities and 25 percent fixed income. Diversification patterns among domestic equity, foreign equity, real estate, and private equity are also strikingly similar. Departures from the norm are typically small and getting smaller. It looks like herding to us.

When we look across the spectrum of institutional investment portfolios, we can often detect the influence of a particular advisor or consultant. It is manifest not only in typical equity allocations but in the role of bonds, the number and style of active managers, the use of passive investment, diversification strategies, and the use of alternative investments. Should policy prescriptions vary largely by advisor or by client circumstance? If investment policy advice varies more by advisor, is it not more art than science?

Questionable resource allocation. Institutional investors know things that should help establish priorities and dictate resource allocation in managing a portfolio. One is that asset allocation policy is the overwhelming determinant of long-run return. Another is that investors generally don't beat the market; it beats them. One might, therefore, expect institutional investors to devote significant resources to investment policy research relative to the resources expended trying to beat the market. But in whatever way we might measure the balance—by staff time or fee expenditures— institutions allocate much more of their resources to active management than to policy research. The allocation of resources is inconsistent with common investment knowledge.

Diagnosis

Four people—one in Mumbai, one in Tokyo, one in Berlin, and one in Los Angeles— enter a doctor's office or hospital complaining of the same symptoms. Unknown to any of the four at the outset, the symptoms indicate appendicitis. In all cases, physicians will listen to the symptoms and then examine the patients. Many problems are ruled out, and a similar battery of tests is ordered by each of the physicians. In relatively short order, all four physicians, following standard medical practice, will almost certainly diagnose appendicitis. Moreover, they are all likely to arrive at the same conclusion as to whether and when to operate. And when they do operate, all will execute the procedure in the same fashion. This describes the application of a well-developed professional method.

Practitioners lack a professional method for investment policy development. We have a rich literature and many eager practitioners but nothing that resembles a universally accepted, systematic application of process and accumulated knowledge to solve a common social science problem.

A Call for Papers

Reflection on the state of investment policy research leads us to raise several questions:

- If theory is impractical, can it be considered good theory?
- Alternatively, if formulation of rational investment policy is stymied by a thicket of agency issues, should the structure and governance of investing institutions be reformed?
- If a class of funds occupies a distinct investment policy habitat, irrespective of variation in circumstance, what accounts for the selection of habitat? In other words, how does the herd determine where to locate itself?
- If decision makers are unable to ascribe utility to hypothetical future outcomes many years into the future when they don't have an inkling of the larger context in which those outcomes might occur, are multiperiod simulation models even relevant?
- Practitioners know how to evaluate portfolio performance. How does one evaluate the performance of an investment policy?
- Is it feasible to create a professional method for the development of investment policy? What would it look like?
- What role does CFA Institute have in advancing a professional method?

We would like to narrow the gap between theory and practice in investment policy research. In this spirit, we call for papers that might inform practitioners' thinking on the questions raised here and help ensure that, as a profession, we move in the direction of more science, less art in deciding institutional investment policy.

Exploring Market Macro-Inefficiency: Call for Papers
September/October 2007, Vol. 63, No. 5:8

The swoon of the U.S. housing market makes me wonder whether Paul Samuelson's "dictum" isn't becoming Robert Shiller's legacy.

Some years ago, renowned economist Paul Samuelson observed that, although markets are largely micro-efficient, they are, at the same time, macro-inefficient. The idea is that the pricing of individual securities exhibits a considerable degree of efficiency but markets, as aggregations of prices, can and do exhibit irrational pricing—the stuff of bubbles. The finance literature sometimes refers to this seeming paradox as "Samuelson's dictum."[10]

For his part, Robert Shiller of Yale University famously pronounced the stock market acutely overvalued during the bubble of the late 1990s. His *Irrational Exuberance* hit bookstore shelves just before the market broke. He was dead right, of course. His simple P/E chart for the S&P 500 Index remains for many of us an icon of the era.

More recently, Shiller made the case that a bubble was forming in the housing market in the United States. His data indicate that real housing prices increased by more than 60 percent between 1997 and 2005. At the same time, he showed that the sharp increase cannot be explained by such factors as trends in building costs, interest rates, or population. Although it is far too soon to write the history of the sharp rise in housing prices observed in the late 1990s and early 2000s, this phenomenon may ultimately go down as another notorious case of widespread irrational pricing.[11]

The regularity with which bubbles arise in modern markets suggests several themes we hope to explore in future issues of the FAJ. For example:

What theory underlies chronic macro-inefficiency? Is macro-inefficiency a by-product of business-cycle economics, is it purely behavioral, or is it a combination of the two?

- Is empirical evidence for macro-inefficiency anecdotal or robust?
- Are instances of macro-inefficiency one and the same as bubbles? Or does macro-inefficiency ebb and flow on a smaller scale?
- Can investors exploit macro-inefficiencies? Or are they left to ride out bubbles or simply guess at turning points?
- What does chronic macro-inefficiency imply for investment policy? On the one hand, stock picking has always been a respectable form of active investment, even with its efficacy in question. On the other hand, anything resembling "market timing" has been dogmatically avoided by the institutional investment establishment. Is it time to revisit this doctrine?
- Are investors' time horizons sufficiently long to enable them to live with active strategies based on perceived macro-mispricing? Does tactical asset allocation (TAA) provide sufficient breadth to be an attractive investment strategy?
- What risk control strategies are best suited for TAA? Alternatively, what is the best way to insulate a portfolio from bubbles?
- Can developments in financial institutions, markets, or instruments ameliorate macro-inefficiencies? Are there aspects of deregulation that might have the same effect?

We are soliciting papers that address these timely issues. A better understanding of them would be a valuable addition to our body of knowledge.

NOTES

1. Andrew W. Lo, "Risk Management for Hedge Funds: Introduction and Overview," *Financial Analysts Journal*, vol. 57, no. 6 (November/December 2001):16–33

2. Richard M. Ennis, "Parsimonious Asset Allocation," *Financial Analysts Journal*, vol. 65, no. 3 (May/June 2009):6–10

3. See Hurley, Mark P., Sharon I. Meers, Ben J. Bornstein, and Neil R. Strumingher. 1995. "The Coming Evolution of the Investment Management Industry: Opportunities and Strategies." Investment Management Industry Group, Goldman Sachs (October).

4. Real estate is represented by the Dow Jones U.S. Select REIT Index, hedge funds by the HFRI Fund of Funds Composite Index, and private equity by an equal-weighted average of the returns of six private equity funds with listed shares.

5. See, for example, Clifford S. Asness, Robert J. Krail, and John M. Liew, "Do Hedge Funds Hedge?" *Journal of Portfolio Management*, vol. 28, no. 1 (Fall 2001):6–19.

6. See Richard M. Ennis, "The Case for Whole-Stock Portfolios," *Journal of Portfolio Management* (Spring 2001):17–26.

7. Lawrence Fisher and James H. Lorie, "Rates of Return on Investment Common Stocks: The Year-by-Year Record, 1926–1965," *Journal of Business* (July 1968):291–316

8. See "Optimal Investment Policies for University Endowment Funds," ch. 21 in Merton's *Continuous-Time Finance* (Malden, MA: Blackwell, 1992).

9. Fischer Black, "The Tax Consequences of Long-Run Pension Policy," *Financial Analysts Journal* (July/August 1980):21–28.

10. See, for example, Jeeman Jung and Robert Shiller, "Samuelson's Dictum and the Stock Market," *Economic Inquiry*, vol. 43, no. 2 (April 2005):221–228.

11. Robert Shiller, *Irrational Exuberance*, 2nd edition (New York: Doubleday, 2005)

ACKNOWLEDGMENTS

Colin Ennis and Ryan Ennis encouraged me to undertake the project, and Ryan coached me along the way to completion. Rodney Sullivan provided encouragement, support and helpful comments. Charley Ellis and John O'Brien helped with ancient history. In taking license with the academic concept of risk tolerance in my discussion of it, I consulted Bill Sharpe, who is *not* responsible for what I wrote. Steve Sexauer prodded me to include an extended discussion of my thinking about investment policy that appears as an appendix. Joanne Hickman Dodd made helpful suggestions. Former colleagues, now with Aon Investment Consulting, were helpful in a number of ways. Steve Cummings helped me with EnnisKnupp history. P.J. Kelly offered a number of suggestions to shape the story. Steve Voss helped fill the void in my understanding of investment practice that developed during the years since my retirement. Sudhakar ("Doc") Attaluri conjured analytical and statistical results, as needed. *Financial Analysts Journal* was generous in granting permission to reprint my editorials. Mike Valentino edited the book. Leah Spiro provided helpful editorial suggestions. David Wogahn of Authorimprints made publication a breeze. Jim Knupp, of course, played a key role in the creation and success of our firm, absent which there would be no story to tell. Sally cheered me on and made sure I got the important facts right.

Life was all about cars and racing in the author's teenage years.

Sally Hinton, at about the time the author discovered her in a college algebra class, and the author at about the same time

The brothers of Phi Delta Psi (author: front, center)

Harry Markowitz introduced the author
to finance theory at UCLA.

Salim ("Cy") Lewis, legendary Managing Partner of Bear
Stearns, taught the author the fine points of block trading.

Mentors and life-long friends: John O'Brien (above left), William Sharpe (above right), and Fischer Black (directly above)

Stuart Gassel, long-time head of A.G.
Becker's Funds Evaluation Group

At Becker (left to right), Jim Knupp, Jack Marco
(later of Marco Consulting) and Robb Rowe

"Professor" Gil Beebower teaching a class at Becker

WE ARE PLEASED TO ANNOUNCE THE FORMATION OF

Ennis, Knupp & Gold
INCORPORATED

RICHARD M. ENNIS, C.F.A.   JAMES F. KNUPP

RONALD A. GOLD

69 WEST WASHINGTON STREET

SUITE 3105   TELEPHONE

CHICAGO, ILLINOIS 60602   (312) 263-4300

Ennis, Knupp & Gold, Inc., opens for business February 1, 1981

Ron Gold, the author and Jim Knupp (left to right)
in the early days of Ennis, Knupp & Gold, Inc.

A company outing in the early days of EnnisKnupp

Sally and Richard hosting an EnnisKnupp holiday party

ENNIS, KNUPP & ASSOCIATES

10 SOUTH RIVERSIDE PLAZA · CHICAGO

For most of its history EnnisKnupp operated from a single office located on the Chicago River, directly opposite the Chicago Mercantile Exchange, a client of the firm.

As Editor of *Financial Analysts Journal*, the author is the guest of the CFA Society Japan

The Sanibel poolroom, modeled after *Harry's*

Sally and Richard, *en corte,* while doing the tango

Family gathering on the Sanibel beach,
at the author's home there

CPSIA information can be obtained
at www.ICGtesting.com
Printed in the USA
BVHW011923090819
555551BV00003B/9/P